On the Edge

A collection of 17 hard-hitting Christian monologs for youth

STEVEN

D1295388

MERIWETHER PUBLISHING LTD.
Colorado Springs, Colorado

Meriwether Publishing Ltd., Publisher
PO Box 7710
Colorado Springs, CO 80933-7710

Editor: Rhonda Wray
Cover design: Jan Melvin

Library of Congress Cataloging-in-Publication Data

James, Steven, 1969-
  On the edge : a collection of 17 hard-hitting Christian monologs for youth / Steven James.--1st ed.
    p. cm.
  Includes index.
  ISBN-13: 978-1-56608-100-X
  ISBN-10: 1-56608-100-9
  1. Drama in Christian education. 2. Christian education of teenagers.
  3. Monologues, American. 4. Monodramas. I. Title.
  BV1534.4.J36 2004
  268'.433--dc22
                    2004022406

1 2 3   04 05 06

Dedication

For Eddy Hall and Carol Duerksen

Thanks and Acknowledgments

Sections of the chapter "The Night I Wrote the Note" appeared previously in the June 1999 issue of *Living with Teenagers*, the October/November 1999 issue of *With: The Magazine for Radical Christian Youth* and in the January/February 2003 issue of *Campus Life*.

Earlier versions of "The Delivery Boy," "Razor's Edge," and "Valley of the Shadow" first appeared in *YouthWalk*. Tim Walker, the editor at *YW*, has been a tremendous encouragement over the years. Thanks, Tim.

My thanks go out to all the editors from these magazines (and many others) whose suggestions and insights have helped improve my stories along the way.

Special thanks to Lauren Vernon, Pam Johnson, Marian Green, Liesl Huhn, Curt Cloninger, Jeff Smith, and Anne Carpenter, who helped me *tremendously* with their insights, questions, critiques, and suggestions on earlier versions of these monologs.

Thanks also to Rhonda Wray, Mark Zapel, and Pamela Harty for working hard to give me the opportunity to write this book. It was an honor and a joy.

Contents

Introduction

"I am the Black Prince."

That's what he told me: "I am the Black Prince."

I'd just finished telling a group of teenagers a story from ancient Egypt about a boy who loved to play the flute. He would sit on a wall near a garden and play all day long. Then one day, he saw this girl walking through the garden and fell in love with her from a distance. He figured she'd never seen him or heard his music, and he wanted more than anything to be with her.

But then, when he found out she was the princess, he gave up all hope of being with her — after all, she was rich and powerful and would never be interested in a poor boy like him. So, he sought out this sorcerer, who changed him into a great and vicious warrior, ruthless and brave. People called him the "Black Prince," for he wore a black cape and rode a steed the color of midnight.

After leading the Egyptian soldiers to an impressive victory, he returned to ask for the hand of the princess in marriage.

But when he proposed, she lowered her eyes. "My heart belongs to another," she told him. "A boy who would sit near my garden and play the flute. I'm sure he never even saw me. A soul so free and alive would never be interested in a princess. Some say he was eaten by crocodiles in the Nile, but I believe he will return to me one day. And if he does, I'll introduce myself and tell him of my undying love. So, though I could marry you, Black Prince, I could never love you."

A shudder rippled down the spine of the Black Prince. "I will not ask you to marry me," he whispered. "I, too, have loved … I too have loved … "

Then the Black Prince rode off on his steed into the desert and was never seen again.[1]

When I finished telling the story, Peter, a high school sophomore, came up to me. He looked around to make sure no one else was listening, then he whispered, "I am the Black Prince."

I nodded. I understood.

Peter had seen himself in the story. It was a mirror for his soul. He entered the story. And so the story became his, for he'd also tried to change who he was to impress others, only to find that they had loved

[1] The story of "The Black Prince" is found in *The Black Prince and Other Egyptian Folk Tales* by Ahmed and Zane Zagloul, 1971, Doubleday & Company, Inc.

1

him the way he was before. I didn't have to tell Peter what the story meant. He knew. And he knew it was his story.

Sure, I could have told those high school students, "Now remember to always be yourself. You don't have to change so that people will like you." And sure, he might have listened to me, but he wouldn't have heard me. At least not with the same ears that heard that story. The words would have bounced off him. Most of the time, our souls are bulletproof to advice, to platitudes, to moralizing. But stories have armor-piercing tips that slice through all of our defenses and imbed themselves in our hearts. Stories touch us deeply because, as we enter them, they enter us.

Stories are the most powerful way to impart truth. Period.

God knew that. That's why he gave us a storybook rather than a theology textbook. The Old Testament prophets knew that. That's why they spoke in riddles, in metaphor, in imagery, and in story. Jesus knew that, too. That's why he chose to become a storyteller rather than a seminary professor. *"Jesus always used stories and illustrations like these when speaking to the crowds. In fact, he never spoke to them without using such parables"* (Matthew 13:34). Using stories to teach spiritual truths mirrors the preferred teaching method of the Master.

Stories help us tackle tough issues. Nathan used a story to confront David about his adultery (2 Samuel 12:1-14); Solomon used a story to help his children think about sexual temptation (Proverbs 7); and Jesus used dozens of stories to shake people out of their comfort zones and into the kingdom of God (see Mark 4:33-34).

Stories work especially well with postmodern teens of today because contemporary students are savvy. They can sense a lecture coming a mile away. They bristle when they're told what to do or what to think. But tell them a story, and you'll have their undivided attention. Especially when the story deals with an issue they've thought about, struggled with, or questioned:

> *"Should I check out those websites my friends told me about?"*
> *"Sometimes I feel like killing myself. What should I do?"*
> *"I just found out Dale's gay. How are we gonna stay friends?"*
> *"Where do I turn when I have a problem I don't want anyone else to know about?"*

2

Stories invite reflection, not argumentation. They encourage listeners to participate, get involved, and then apply the lesson to their own lives. And when stories are honest, they do all this in a way that doesn't turn people off. Instead, stories can bring us face to face with the truth of who we really are — just like the story did for Peter that day, when he realized he was the Black Prince.

Making the Most of This Book

The seventeen stories in this collection tackle tough issues with candor, sensitivity, and honesty. These monologs allow you, the youth leader, to create just the right atmosphere to address modern moral dilemmas with tact, poignancy, and truth.

Each three- to eight-minute monolog includes hints for the director, Scripture references, themes, and discussion ideas (including suggested transitions and follow-up questions) so that you can build an entire lesson around each dramatic performance.

Every monolog in this book deals with modern moral dilemmas that teens of today struggle with. The scripts are thought-provoking, to-the-point, and gut-wrenchingly honest.

Before diving in, take a few minutes to look over the cast, topical, and Scripture verse indices at the end of this book. Become familiar with the topics and verses so you can choose just the right script for your group or event.

Next, check out the tips on performing monologs and working with teen actors (included in the following pages). You'll find lots of helpful information that will save you tons of time and energy later on.

Finally, consider how you want this monolog to fit in with the rest of your lesson or presentation. You may wish to use the drama either to spark interest prior to the teaching time, or to accentuate the worship and application portion of the service after your message. (Please note — most of the dramas in this book present a problem rather than a solution and aren't meant to stand entirely on their own without some type of message or follow-up discussion.)

You could also present a series of lessons to your students by using a different drama each week. Or you could choose three to four monologs to use during a weekend retreat, summer camp, mission trip, or lock-in. You could even present a whole evening of monologs for youth and their parents entitled, "On the Edge: An Honest Look at Life." Include a discussion time afterward with students and parents tackling these tough problems and working out practical, biblical ways to address them in their own lives.

Tips on Performing Monologs

A monolog is a story told from the perspective of one of the characters within the story. Monologs tend to be very personal and informal. And because of that, they can be very disarming. They're real. They're raw. They're transformational.

Most often, monologs are told from the point of view of one of the people in a story, but monologs could also be presented from the perspective of an object, a spiritual entity (such as an angel or a demon), or an animal. All of the monologs in this collection are told from the point of view of a teenage guy or girl.

Monologs mirror actual language. Because of that, they aren't written in complete, well-structured, complex sentences. Why not? Because we don't talk in complete, well-structured, complex sentences! We talk in spurts, in jumbles, and in bursts and wipeouts and mumbles and murmurs and sighs and grunts as we feel out which words to say and as we try to formulate and organize our thoughts.

We stumble and correct ourselves.

We pause and reflect.

We backtrack.

Sometimes we seem to wander off on tangents (as we're temporarily distracted), and then we recover and get back to the main point again. That's how we talk. So, as a result, good monologs sound like that. They aren't sermons in disguise. They aren't long, boring, eloquent soliloquies in proper-sounding Elizabethan English.

Effective monologs are a little rough around the edges. They're not polished to a smooth, glassy sheen. You might get a splinter handling them. And that's good. 'Cause that's what happens when you get up close to the truth — you poke at it, and it pokes back.

The subtlety of good monologs is that the back and forth, wandering-type narrative *is* carefully woven together, even though it may sound random. In this way, monologs reflect natural dialog and storytelling but eliminate all extraneous material so that they have a greater impact on the audience.

Some people have spent lots of time and ink trying to define and clarify the difference between acting and storytelling. Frankly, I think there are a lot more similarities than differences, so I'll leave the hair-splitting to others. Whatever your views, monologs land somewhere in the gray area between telling a story and acting one out.

Actors often focus on *why* they're onstage or what's *motivating them* to speak. Storytellers tend to focus more on *what* they have to say and on *connecting with* this audience this day. So, be aware that these monologs lie in that hard-to-categorize area between the stage and the front porch, between the theater and the campfire. Enjoy them for what they are, whatever you decide to call them.

Many times I've seen monologs fall flat because the actor simply stands onstage and talks. Talks, talks, talks.

Because no one else is onstage to interact with him, and there are no changes of scenery, this can get old and lame pretty quickly.

One of the secrets to performing effective monologs is to find a way to translate emotion into action. For example, rather than standing onstage trying to look or "act" nervous, do something that expresses or shows nervousness: pace, fidget, fumble with your keys, repeatedly stuff your hands in your pockets and then pull them out again, bite your lower lip, wring your hands, avoid eye contact with the audience, stare at the floor, crack your knuckles ... The key is to show that you're nervous. Rather than thinking *I'm gonna act nervous,* try to step into the shoes of someone who is *already* nervous, and then act naturally. Always search for a physical way of expressing emotion rather than just standing there "emoting."

When actors and directors talk about "motivation," they're referring to the desires that drive the character an actor is portraying. What does that person want? Why is she onstage anyway? What is she hoping to accomplish? All of these motivations are action-oriented, not emotion-oriented. Rather than telling your actor to be happy or sad or angry or confused, help him step into the character and understand why he's feeling that way and *what he hopes to accomplish* by the end of the drama.

Be aware that all of your gestures should be purposeful, genuine, and relevant to the piece. If you only have a few movements, they'll have more of an impact and not become muted or lost in the static of your constant, mindless movement.

Also, whenever you shift from one topic to another, it's natural to also shift to another stance, activity, or gesture; or to change the focus of your gaze and attention. As monologs flip back and forth between two, three, or even four story lines, use these changes in focus or posture to re-orient your audience to where you are and what you're talking about.

Prop manipulation and blocking (i.e., movement) give you an excuse to do something (i.e., manipulate the prop!) as well as to pause at certain points in the story. You can use these pauses to your advantage to add emphasis to what you're saying or to let the words you've just said sink in a little more.

Remember that your character, within the context of the story, is saying his lines for the first time. You may have practiced them a hundred times, but the words need to sound fresh and alive to the audience. Even though you know the whole script already, the character you're portraying doesn't know what he's going to say next. For him the future hasn't happened yet, the story hasn't played itself out. *You* know the story from the outside in; he only knows it from the inside out. So, to become more believable, try to really see the story through your character's eyes, and then act accordingly.

Use the space onstage. Look for ways of exploring different levels (low, medium, and high) as you develop your piece. Remember:

- Gestures should look natural to the audience and feel natural to you. If you practice certain ways of moving and they end up looking "canned," the monolog won't look genuine.
- Your facial expressions should flow from what you're experiencing as you perform your piece. The more you try to show "what the character should be feeling," the more you'll appear to overact and you'll look cheesy.

Overall, be honest. Believe in your piece. Step into your character, and then respond naturally and honestly, however he or she would respond. Don't just *act* like you care about what's happening to your character — care. When your audience sees that, they'll care, too.

Tips on Directing Teen Actors

Teens of today live busy lives. They're often overcommitted, stressed out, and functioning on too little sleep. If you recruit a student to perform one of these monologs, make sure that he or she has the time, energy, motivation, and ability to see it through. Dramas have fallen into disfavor in some churches because they haven't been well prepared or well performed. Don't let that happen at your church.

Keep in mind that the egos of teen actors are fragile. Be as positive and encouraging as you can be. Many people who enjoy acting and getting involved in theater tend to be shy in front of small groups, but more at ease in front of larger audiences. That means they may be easily intimidated rehearsing a monolog in front of you or just a few other people. Consequently, you must do all you can to help them relax and feel at ease. (The opposite is also true. You may have some students who are great in rehearsals, but when the auditorium is full of actual people, they freeze up.) It is imperative that you get to know your students and try to help them each individually deal with their own specific anxieties.

Don't dwell on the negative and nitpick when you're directing dramas or monologs. It's often more effective to simply say, "What did you think of that? How did it feel to you?" than to come down hard on someone. Your actor will often point out the very things you noticed, but when it comes from him, it won't seem like you're getting on his case. Instead, notice the things he did well. For example, you might say, "I really liked it when you threw your books into your backpack and then pounded it with your fist. It's great when you can find actions that reflect the feelings of the characters." This way, you can encourage him as well as teach him what's effective.

Make sure your students show up for rehearsals and are prepared to present their pieces. You'll also need to have the courage and tact to tell a student that he or she simply isn't ready, if that's the case.

Don't feel too tied to the script. Some playwrights are very touchy (and in some cases, justifiably so) about people changing the wording of their scripts. I believe that because of the interpersonal aspect of storytelling, storytellers need to be able to use language that's comfortable and natural for them. I feel it's vital that the script and the performer mesh well together.

So, even though great care has been taken in crafting the language of the stories in this collection, you may find that sometimes a slightly different wording sounds more natural to you. Feel free to make minor editorial changes to the scripts in this book. I don't mind if you change a few phrases if it helps the piece sound more natural for the actor or actress who is performing it. You may wish to leave out a joke that wouldn't make sense to your listeners, or delete a phrase that might be misunderstood. (However, permission is not granted to alter the stories in such a way that you change the meaning or overall moral intent of the story.)

If you choose to direct the dramas by yourself, you may wish to recruit another youth leader of the opposite sex to be present at rehearsals so that you're not alone with one of the students. This will help avoid any appearance of impropriety. The other leader could help with coordinating props, microphones, or any other technical needs.

Finally, let me just say it — use the people who have the skills to act. You'd never let someone preach or sing a solo just because he *wanted* to. First, you'd want to make sure he had the skills and abilities to do so. For some reason, many church drama directors feel that they have to cast certain students just because those students want to act or be in a production. Don't fall into this trap, especially when you're presenting monologs! In monologs, you need to make sure that the actor or actress is skilled enough *to carry the entire story.* There's no one else there to bail him or her out or save the show. Use the gifted students. And don't ever feel bad about it.

1. No Thanks

Summary:

Bruce's friends keep inviting him to youth group events, but from what he's seen so far, he's just not interested in what Christianity has to offer.

Purpose:

Use this drama to spark a discussion on hypocrisy, being real when you share your faith with others, or repenting of "little" sins. This drama would work great for igniting a frank discussion with your youth group about how they appear to the "outside" world.

Time:

Three to four minutes

Props/Set:

A can of soda, a chair

Topics:

Authenticity, counterfeit spirituality, hypocrisy, Jesus, masks, witnessing

Cast:

You're Bruce, a seventeen-year-old guy who doesn't go to church or know much about Christianity. You have a bunch of Christian friends and have been turned off by some of the things you've seen them do and say.

Notes:

Encourage Bruce to appear likeable, not resentful or bitter. He's not angry at anyone in particular, he's just not interested in the version of Christianity to which he's been exposed. The can of soda represents the hollowness and emptiness of the form of Christianity Bruce has seen.

Notes for the Actor

Bring a can of soda On-stage with you and drink it as you deliver this monolog.

Have fun with this early stuff. You want the audience to be on your side. Feel free to add something relevant to your group, if appropriate.

When you get to the lines about the ski trip, be sure you don't sound too negative. You want the audience to really see these events through your eyes.

You're not making fun of Jesus in this section, you just don't really understand who he is or what any of this has to do with you.

BRUCE: So this friend of mine — Justin — he's always inviting me to these youth group things at his church. And I gotta admit, sometimes they can be pretty cool. Once we had this lock-in where we stayed up all night and went swimming at the YMCA … we had a belly-flop contest at, like, five a.m. … off the high dive. The kid who won weighed like three hundred pounds. He was this all-state tackle in football … Shamu.

Another time we duct-taped his youth pastor to the wall and threw cafeteria food at him. I never knew mystery meat could stick so well to a goatee …

Oh, and then one time they rented this wood chipper and we fed watermelons into it and shot 'em at the kids who lost this pie-eating contest. It was cool. Gross — but very cool.

I even went on this ski trip with 'em last winter. That was cool, too — except for one thing. They had, like, this skit night or something where all these different youth groups did little plays and then they had this guy stand up to talk about God.

Now, I got nothing against God and all that, but I didn't grow up going to church or anything. So the whole thing was … well … pretty interesting. I mean, almost all of their skits showed these kids partying or drinking and then some girl has to choose if she wants to go to the party or sit and read her Bible.

OK — tough choice there.

And then, at the end of the skit, there's always this car accident — every skit has a car accident — and everyone dies and all the people who chose to sit and read their Bibles go to heaven, where I guess they get to do it forever. And they all, like, kneel down and pray to some guy wearing a wig and a dress — I think it's supposed to be Jesus or Buddha or someone. And all the kids who chose to have fun go to … well, you get the picture.

Like I said, pretty interesting.

And then they ask you if you'd like to give up drinking, smoking, and sleeping with your girlfriend so you can go and read your Bible with the guy in the dress.

So I'm sitting there watching all this happen and I'm thinking, "OK, is this some kind of trick question? Did I miss something here? Why would anyone choose that?"

But a few kids did. They went up front and everyone clapped and Justin — the friend of mine who invited me — he nudges me and he's like, "Hey, what do you think? I'll walk up there with you if you want — "

And he was serious.

So I'm like, "Um, no thanks. Not tonight."

And he smiles and pats me on the back. "OK, maybe next week."

And it's always the same stuff: smoking, drinking, and having sex. It's like those are the three things my friends are against. Their skits never bring up all the stuff they do — like talking about people behind their backs, looking down on others, picking on 'em, leaving kids out who don't look like them, gossiping, pretending they're better than others, copying homework at school, holding grudges, you know. All that stuff.

But I guess that stuff would hit a little too close to home.

Maybe there's more to Christianity than all that — than lock-ins and food wars and skits about car wrecks. I don't know. But I need something more real than that in my life.

Notes for the Actor

You're clueless. You just don't understand the message of Christianity because it wasn't clearly explained to you.

Here's where the drama hits home to the "churched" kids in your group, because these are the things they do, but don't like to talk about.

Notes for the Actor

When you're done with the monolog, take one final gulp of soda, crumple up the can, shake your head, and walk Off-stage. Just let everything sink in as the lights fade out.

More significant.

Anyway, that's why I don't go to his youth group meetings anymore. I'm just not interested in that kind of religion.

Ideas for the Speaker:

(As BRUCE exits, walk On-stage and face the audience. Then, as the lights come back up, say something like ...)

Ever wonder what it would be like to take a look at our group from the outside in? What would you see? Just lock-ins and food wars and skits about car wrecks? Is that it? Or would you see Jesus? Would you see people who are so in love with him that they just can't help but let it out? Or would you see people who are more concerned about their image, reputation, and appearance? Would you see people so in love with Jesus that they actually lived out their faith in real ways? Or so in love with themselves that they don't put his words into practice at all?

And what about all those uncomfortable little sins that the guy in the drama noticed — talking about people behind their backs, looking down on others, picking on them, leaving kids out who don't look like you, gossiping, pretending you're better than others, copying homework at school, holding grudges — was he right? Would that stuff hit a little too close to home?

As Jesus said once, *"So why do you call me 'Lord,' when you won't obey me?" (Luke 6:46).*

Let's take a few minutes to pray. Let's ask God to help us live genuine, caring, real lives; lives honest enough to express our need for him. Someone once said, "The main thing is keeping the main thing the main thing." Let's pray that the main thing — the love and forgiveness of God for a lost and dying world — would shine through us in all we do. *(Prayer follows.)*

Verses to Check Out:

- *"I passed on to you what was most important and what had also been passed on to me — that Christ died for our sins, just as the Scriptures said" (1 Corinthians 15:3).*
- *"Search me, O God, and know my heart; test me and know my thoughts" (Psalm 139:23).*
- *"We are made right in God's sight when we trust in Jesus Christ to take away our sins. And we all can be saved in this same way, no matter who we are or what we have done" (Romans 3:22).*

2. Bread Crumbs

Summary:

Two years ago, when Liz found out she was pregnant, she decided to get an abortion — until a story she'd heard as a little girl gave her the courage to change her mind.

Purpose:

Use this drama to bring up the issue of abortion in an honest and life-affirming way.

Time:

Five to six minutes

Props/Set:

Stale bread for Liz to crumble and toss off to the side of the stage, a park bench for her to sit on

Topics:

Abortion, choices, courage, life, maturity, pregnancy, second chances

Cast:

You're Liz, an eighteen-year-old girl who chose to keep your baby when you found out you were pregnant two years ago. As the scene opens, you're sitting on a park bench feeding some birds. You've made some bad choices but have finally gotten the guts to do what's right, even when it's tough. Currently, you're living with a friend in an apartment.

Notes:

Listen for pauses, especially during the moments when Liz realizes something. Coach your actress to be sensitive and vulnerable so that the audience can identify with her, but also to be bold and firm enough to stand up for her convictions.

LIZ: Sometimes I come here to the park. To feed the birds. They like stale bread crumbs. At least that's what someone told me once ... *(Pause)*

When I was little, my mom told me this story about these two kids — Hansel and Gretel. You've probably heard it. Anyway, in the story, their mom convinces their dad to leave 'em in the woods — abandon 'em, you know — 'cause she doesn't want to take care of 'em anymore.

So he goes along with the idea, and the kids leave rocks all along the trail and find their way home. So he tries again and they didn't have enough time to gather up rocks, so they bring a loaf of bread and use bread crumbs. But the birds eat the bread crumbs, and the two kids end up at the witch's house. And this witch lures 'em inside. You remember: "Nibble, nibble like a mouse; who's that nibbling at my house?" Anyway. The whole routine. Finally, they trick the witch, roast her, find their way home — where their mom has since died — their dad says he's sorry, and they all live happily ever after. The end.

(After a beat) Yeah, right.

I don't get it. Like, why would Hansel and Gretel keep letting their dad abandon 'em in the forest? I mean, how come they don't catch on? And what about the ending? How did they find their way back home without the bread crumbs? And most of all, the thing I don't understand — and didn't, even when I was a kid — was how the parents could ever plan to kill their kids in the first place just because it wasn't convenient having 'em around. What kind of parents are those? I mean, what is *that* about? *(Pause)*

Notes for the Actress

As the lights come up, crumble up some little pieces of bread and toss them across the stage. Then look up at the audience and begin.

Sit while you tell the fairy tale. Toss crumbs as you talk about it.

Don't spend too much time on the fairy tale. You want to remind people of the story without beating them over the head with it.

It should be a bit of a surprise to the audience when you say, "Yeah, right."

Stand up and walk around the bench as you ask the questions. Let the audience really think about these questions before you move on with the monolog.

Notes for the Actress

Here is another surprise — you had to ask yourself the same question. You could sit for this section.

This section about telling your boyfriend is intense. Deliver it facing the audience eye to eye. Stand and walk again.

Pause after saying the line "He says he'll pay for it." Let that sink in. Here you're trying to really justify your decision. You're telling yourself this will solve everything, but you know it won't, not really.

Avert eye contact during this section. You're ashamed of what you were about to do just because it was convenient.

But then, about two years ago, I found out.

You see, my boyfriend and I had been together for about five months, and … well, you know … We both wanted to hook up, so we started hanging out at his house after school, before his parents got home.

It was about two months after that when I found out.

I almost died when the test came back positive. I mean, I was only sixteen. And I was gonna have a baby! My life was totally over.

So I tell my boyfriend, and he gets all mad like it was my fault or something. And then he's like, "How do you know it's mine?" He actually asked me if I knew it was his …

"It couldn't have been anyone else's!" I said.

And then he's like, "Well, how much is it gonna cost?" That's exactly what he said: "How much is it gonna cost?"

And I'm like, "How much is what gonna cost?"

"You know, to get it taken care of," he says.

So I tell him, and he says he'll pay for it.

I couldn't have a baby. I'm not old enough to have a baby. It was the only thing I could do. You understand, right? I picked up the money and headed to the clinic. All I had to do was show up with the cash and they'd take care of everything.

Solve everything.

Terminate the pregnancy.

And it all sounded so reasonable. It all seemed to make so much sense. It was all so convenient.

But then, as I was heading to the clinic, I walked past this park. And I saw these birds flying overhead, swooping down. You know, eating something. Picking something up from the grass. Bread crumbs. And I remembered.

Children. Lost in the woods. Left there to die. By their parents.

With no bread-crumb trail to follow back home.

A mother and a father who decide to leave their kids in the dark forest. Leave 'em to the witch ... Because it just wasn't convenient having 'em around ...

(With conviction) I never made it to the clinic that day.

I kept my baby. She's a girl. Susan Lynn Collins. And my boyfriend left me — right after I gave him his money back. And the people at school laughed at me and whispered behind my back. And I heard the things they were saying. And then I had to quit going to classes altogether and get a job. My parents still haven't forgiven me ...

They make "happily ever after" sound so easy in the story. But it's not easy. It's tough ... It's really tough.

Leaving your kid in the dark forest?

No, I just couldn't do it. That fairy tale has been around long enough. And if we're old enough to enter the story, we're old enough to write a better ending ... and a better beginning. *(Pause for a beat.)*

I take Susan on walks. Here in the park. Where the birds fly. And swoop and land. Eating bread crumbs. She watches 'em, and points and laughs. She loves to watch the birds. Then I hold her and I hug her and I take her back home again.

Notes for the Actress

Stand and look around the park as you talk about walking through it. Look at your bread crumbs as you talk about the birds and about remembering.

It hasn't been easy keeping your baby. People have judged you and that hurts. But deep down you know you made the right decision.

Here, you're boldly calling people to make the right choice. Deliver these lines with conviction, then break off a piece of bread and toss it across the stage.

17

> **Notes for the Actress**
>
> Point over the audience's heads to your (unseen) daughter when you say "She's the blonde one." Then kneel and smile. Freeze as the stage lights slowly fade to black.

She's the blonde one. There. In the sandbox. C'mon, Susan! Come to Mommy. It's time to go home!

Ideas for the Speaker:

(You could address your comments specifically to those students who have had to face the choice of whether or not to have an abortion, but that might only be a small percentage of your listeners. Instead, to draw a broader application from this monolog, walk On-stage as LIZ exits and face the audience. Then, as the lights come back up, say something like …)

Wouldn't it be great if doing the right thing were easy? If it made sense all the time and helped us stay popular? Trouble is, real life doesn't always work like that. It hurts and it's messy and sometimes no one is there when you need them the most.

It takes a lot of guts to do what's right and not just what's convenient.

Whatever mistakes you've made in your past, God can forgive. Whatever wounds you carry, God can heal. He cares about all those lonely times and those tough times and those confusing times. And he offers to help you through them — to give you the strength and comfort and forgiveness you need.

Every word of his is a bread crumb leading you back home. Will you follow them?

The Bible says that our God is the "God of all comfort" and the "Father of compassion" (see 2 Corinthians 1:3–7, NIV). Today I'd like to give you the chance to bring something to God, to ask him for comfort and compassion. Whatever decisions you've had to face, whatever burdens you might be carrying, God cares, and he can set you on the right road again. *(If desired, offer to pray for kids individually or in small groups.)*

Verses to Check Out:

- *"You made all the delicate, inner parts of my body and knit me together in my mother's womb"* (Psalm 139:13).
- *"Anyone who welcomes a little child like this on my behalf welcomes me, and anyone who welcomes me welcomes my Father who sent me"* (Mark 9:37).
- *"Children are a gift from the LORD; they are a reward from him"* (Psalm 127:3).
- *"What is wrong cannot be righted. What is missing cannot be recovered"* (Ecclesiastes 1:15).

3. The Pictures

Summary:
When Eric began looking at internet pornography, he didn't think it would affect him at all — but now, he's starting to feel the consequences.

Purpose:
Use this powerful drama to discuss pornography, lust, and flirting with sin.

Time:
Three minutes

Props/Set:
A laptop computer, a chair

Topics:
Addictions, choices, consequences, lust, pornography, regrets, relationships, sex, temptation, traps

Cast:
You're Eric, an eighteen-year-old guy who's become addicted to pornography. As a result, you've lost your girlfriend and your innocence. Now you don't even want to look at the pictures anymore, but you can't help it. You're trapped and you keep going back for more, even though it's destroying you.

Notes:
Pornography is a huge industry and a giant trap for many guys, yet no one seems to be talking about it. This script gives you the chance to discuss this important social and moral issue. This intense drama doesn't depend on lurid descriptions for its impact, but rather it uses subtle suggestions and understatement. Encourage your actor to really be aware of his pauses, to let the impact of his words reach the listeners. As he types on his laptop, have him actually use the computer rather than just pretend to do so. It'll add authenticity to the drama.

ERIC: It started small.

Just checking out a few sites on the Web. Sites I'd heard about from my friends. I mean, it was easy to get into 'em. Totally easy.

I did it at night while my parents were asleep upstairs. Then I just, you know, deleted the sites from the computer's history when I was done.

And I gotta say, some of the stuff I saw really shocked me. Pretty disgusting ...

But some of the pictures ... Well, I guess they kinda lodged in my brain. I found myself thinking about 'em during class ... and at work ... and when I was alone with my girlfriend. And it was hard not to compare her to the girls in the pictures — even though I knew they were all fake and Photoshopped and doctored up and everything.

And to be honest, there wasn't really any comparison. I mean, she's nice enough, Katy is. And she's cute and everything ... but ... well ... Anyway, that's when I started going online more and more. Downloading some of the pictures, you know. Printing em out and taking 'em up to my room.

And it didn't take me long to realize that some of the pictures I'd seen at first, you know — back when I first logged onto those sites — were pretty mild. And the stuff that used to really shock me, well, it didn't faze me that much anymore. Didn't even interest me anymore.

No one knew about it. I wasn't hurting anyone. And I told myself it was something I could control, you know. Stop at any time. But I didn't ... I didn't stop.

Notes for the Actor

When the lights come up, you're seated On-stage, typing on a laptop computer. Then you look up at the audience and begin your lines.

As you remember some of the pictures, you're drawn into the images. You can't escape them.

In your mind you're comparing Katy to the pictures, and she doesn't measure up.

You're so used to it now that nothing surprises you — or fulfills you.

21

Notes for the Actor

Pause after saying that you wanted to try stuff with Katy. Let that sink in for a moment. That's a pretty intense line.

You're just using these insults as a way to avoid admitting your addiction.

After saying "Back to just me and the pictures," pause and stare at the computer screen.

After finishing your lines, fold up your laptop, pick it up, and exit. Fade to black.

So then — I told you about Katy, right? — well, after seeing the pictures, they gave me ideas. The pictures did. So when we were alone together ... Well, I wanted to try stuff with her. Stuff I'd seen ...

Then one night last week when we were together, she said she didn't want to see me anymore. She was scared of how I was changing. That's how she put it: "You're not the same guy anymore." She was shaking when she said it.

"I'm not changing," I told her. "I'm still the same."

And then she starts crying and I didn't know what to do but just get mad. So I told her how stupid she was being and how I didn't want to see her anymore anyhow 'cause she was ugly and fat and I could do a lot better than her anyway.

So now it's back to just me and the pictures.

And I wish I could turn 'em off and start over. I wish there was a way to stop, because I don't even enjoy it anymore. I don't like what the pictures do to me.

I don't like what I've become. I mean, she was right. I am changing. And I can't stop it.

I wonder if anyone else has ever had this problem, too ...

Ideas for the Speaker:

(As ERIC exits, walk On-stage and face the audience. Then, as the lights come back up, divide your students into discussion groups of three to five people and discuss why pornography is such a trap for so many people.)

- Why don't we talk about lust and pornography that much?
- What can be done about it?
- What practical steps can we take to avoid getting lured in?

- Girls aren't typically as attracted to pornography as guys are. What parallel is there in the lives of girls to this struggle in the lives of guys?
- Read Matthew 5:28–29. How does verse 28 relate to pornography? What do you think Jesus meant by "gouge out your eye"? Was he serious? If it isn't meant to be taken literally, what's his point? If it is meant to be taken literally, why don't we do it? *(Note — In these verses, Jesus is referring to the severe consequences of sin. Sin is so serious to God that we should be radical in the way we deal with it. We shouldn't only avoid the situations and relationships that lead us deeper into sin, but we should purposely and unashamedly remove those influences from our lives. Today, hard-core pornography is only a mouse click away and, like it or not, the problem isn't just gonna go away. Discuss with your students what influences they need to "gouge out" of their lives and how they're going to do it.)*

End by praying for healing for past choices and the peace and freedom that only Christ can bring. Remind your students that *"There is no condemnation for those who belong to Christ Jesus. For the power of the life-giving Spirit has freed you through Christ Jesus from the power of sin that leads to death"* (Romans 8:1–2).

Verses to Check Out:

- *"I say, anyone who even looks at a woman with lust in his eye has already committed adultery with her in his heart. So if your eye — even if it is your good eye — causes you to lust, gouge it out and throw it away. It is better for you to lose one part of your body than for your whole body to be thrown into hell"* (Matthew 5:28–29).
- *"If we say we have no sin, we are only fooling ourselves and refusing to accept the truth. But if we confess our sins to him, he is faithful and just to forgive us and to cleanse us from every wrong"* (1 John 1:8–9).
- *"I made a covenant with my eyes not to look with lust upon a young woman. ... For lust is a shameful sin, a crime that should be punished"* (Job 31:1,11).

23

4. Now I Gotta Choose

Summary:

Eva is confused and wounded by her parents' divorce. She's become hurt and bitter toward them for what she sees as a broken promise.

Purpose:

Use this drama to challenge adults to take their role of parenting more seriously.

Time:

Three to four minutes

Props/Set:

A flower from which Eva can pull petals, a stool (optional)

Topics:

Anger, communication, divorce, family relationships, resentment

Cast:

You're Eva, a fifteen-year-old girl whose parents have decided to get a divorce. You feel frustrated, helpless, and betrayed. You wonder, "Why can't my parents keep their promise to stay together until 'death do us part'?" None of it makes sense to you, and your anger at the whole situation bubbles to the surface in this brief drama.

Notes:

Divorce is culturally accepted in North America. The divorce rate for believers is nearly identical to that of unbelievers, and yet, God hates divorce (see Malachi 2:16). Because this drama is directed especially at adults, it might work best for a parenting seminar, sermon, or conference.

Whenever Eva pulls the petals from the flower she becomes somewhat thoughtful and reflective.

EVA: When I was a kid, my parents talked a lot about keeping your promises. My mom always said, "Don't make a promise that you're not ready to keep."

They love me. ... They love me not. ... They love me. ...

I don't understand divorce. I just don't get it. I mean, my parents weren't perfect or anything. Anyone could tell that. But I mean, they made a promise, right? "Till death do us part." Isn't that what they say at weddings? "Till death do us part?" Well, the last time I checked, they were both alive. But they sure weren't together.

They love me. ... They love me not. ... They love me. ...

What a joke. And now I gotta decide who to live with. Do I go and live with my mom and listen to her complain all the time about how Dad did this and Dad did that and how she never should have married him in the first place and how he lied to her, and the whole thing?

Or do I go and live with Dad and Stacey? Stacey. She's, like, young enough to be my sister. It's a mess. It's all a mess!

All because they couldn't keep their word.

Till death do us part.

They love me not.

And now I gotta choose Dad or Mom. I mean, how am I supposed to know?! Even though they both get on my nerves and neither of 'em is perfect, I want 'em both. I love 'em both! And just because they can't get along, now I gotta choose!

Notes for the Actress

Throughout this drama you'll be pulling petals off a daisy, saying, "They love me. ... They love me not. ... "

You're sick of the whole situation and wish things could go back to normal again.

Say this run-on sentence quickly to show how annoyed you are at the whole situation.

To you, it boils down to this — your parents didn't keep their word.

Even though you're angry, you love 'em both and hate that you have to be the one to choose what to do.

Notes for the Actress

As you do this section, imitate the voices of your parents. Be a little sarcastic as you mock their reasons.

Here you've started to really get angry. You're past trying to understand why they're getting a divorce; you're letting your true feelings come to the surface. Get faster, louder, and angrier as you list these reasons.

After finishing your lines, look at what's left of the flower, then toss it away and walk off the stage as the lights fade to black.

And they make it sound so reasonable:

(As Dad) "We just weren't right for each other."

(As Mom) "Your father and I just couldn't make it work anymore."

(As Dad) "We tried, Eva! But we just drifted apart. I don't know what we ever saw in each other."

(As Mom) "There are some things you just can't forgive. Sometimes someone goes too far. You'll learn that someday. I hope you don't learn it the hard way like I did."

They couldn't make it work?! They're always talking about forgiving and forgetting. Why can't they forgive?

They love me. ... They love me not. ...

Till death do us part. Yeah, right.

Till arguing do us part ... Till "we can't make it work anymore" do us part ... Till "we drift" do us part ... Till "we're tired of forgiving each other" do us part ... Till we get interested in someone else, till our careers become more important to us than our family, till our daughter is fifteen years old and just wants a stable home, do us part.

I don't get it. *(If you have a stool On-stage, kick it over.)*

It's not right and it's not fair. And now I gotta choose.

I mean, who do you trust at a time like this?

26

Ideas for the Speaker:

(This drama could be directed at parents [relating to the issue of divorce] or to students [relating more to the issues of unresolved anger in family relationships]. The following ideas are examples of follow-up thoughts to use if the audience is primarily adults. As EVA exits, walk On-stage and face the audience. Then, as the lights come back up, say something like ...)

Jesus said that when a couple gets married, they become as one person *(see Matthew 19:5–6; see also Paul's reference to divorce in 1 Corinthians 7:10–11)*. So divorce is really like amputating half of yourself. That's why it hurts so bad. That's why it messes up families and kids and society so bad. It's not an easy way out of a tough situation. It's a surgery that God never intended. Divorce is marital suicide. And that's why God hates divorce *(see Malachi 2:16)*.

But make no mistake about God's love for those in troubled marriages. If you're going through a tough time in your marriage, there's help available. *(Mention a pastor, counseling service, or local Christian psychologist.)* Don't take the easy way out. No marriage is easy. It takes guts to work things out God's way.

Let's move on from here — wherever "here" is for you and your spouse — and do the right thing ...

Verses to Check Out:

- *"A man leaves his father and mother and is joined to his wife, and the two are united into one.' Since they are no longer two but one, let no one separate them, for God has joined them together"* (Matthew 19:5–6).
- *"And I tell you this, a man who divorces his wife and marries another commits adultery — unless his wife has been unfaithful"* (Matthew 19:9).
- *"Now, for those who are married I have a command that comes not from me, but from the Lord. A wife must not leave her husband. But if she does leave him, let her remain single or else go back to him. And the husband must not leave his wife"* (1 Corinthians 7:10–11).

5. The Night I Wrote the Note

Summary:

When no one seemed to notice her or care about her, Jolene decided to end her life.

Purpose:

Use this drama to open up a discussion about suicide. It won't provide all the answers to loneliness and despair, but it will give you the opportunity to begin an honest discussion about suicidal thoughts, emptiness, and the ultimate hope that's only found in Jesus.

Time:

Five to six minutes

Props/Set:

Clothes for Jolene (sweaters, dresses, shoes, etc.), a bed or table on which to lay the clothes

Topics:

Brokenness, death, depression, desperation, emptiness, hope, little things, loneliness, suicide

Cast:

You're Jolene, a seventeen-year-old girl who's been feeling trapped, helpless, lonely, and invisible. Finally, you decide suicide is the only way out. You want to live, but you also want to escape the loneliness that you so often feel. You finally give up on life rather than giving it another chance.

Notes:

Jolene is dead. In this monolog, we see her spirit going through her clothes, choosing the outfit she hopes her body will be dressed in at her funeral. The audience doesn't find out why Jolene is looking over her outfits until the very end of the drama.

Help your actress create a deep sense of regret and foreboding in this drama. It's a sad story, and your goal is to make sure it isn't replayed among any of the students at your church.

JOLENE: The night I wrote the note was an ordinary night.

Just like any other night, I guess. Just like every night. I came home from school, did some homework, surfed the Web for a while ... and then I lay down on my bed and just stared at the ceiling.

And waited.

I went downstairs and ate supper and watched TV and waited some more. But nothing happened. Nothing ...

I don't know exactly what did it for me. It wasn't just one thing. It was like a whole series of little things that all ate away at me. I didn't have a lot of friends. My mom was always getting on my case at home, and my dad was never around, and ... I don't know ... it was like my life was woven with a bunch of threads and they were all unraveling. One at a time. Nothing made sense.

Not school. Not home. Nothing ...

Now that I think about it, I guess it was the phone call that I didn't get. That's what did it. *(Sighs.)* I'd heard there was this party, right? And well, I was hoping maybe someone would invite me — Emily or Jessica or Chondra ... or even Justin — so I waited. But no one called. I waited and waited. And finally, I guess I'd waited long enough. ...

So I wrote the note.

Kind of a stupid reason, huh? I just went over to my desk, pulled out a sheet of paper, and picked up a pen. Just like I was writing a shopping list or a birthday card or something. And there, in the quiet of my room, I wrote my final good-bye.

(Thinking, remembering) The words just spilled out of my heart onto the page, like

Notes for the Actress

Your life was normal, but empty. Nothing you did brought you either joy or fulfillment.

Hold up some clothes and look them over.

Finally, you decided you'd had enough.

When you talk about these other students, show us how lonely you feel that you're not part of their group.

Plop down on the bed or chair as you say "Kind of a stupid reason...".

Pause after saying "my final good-bye."

29

Notes for the Actress

Pause again after saying that you knew how and when.

Stand up, pick up more sweaters, and shuffle through them as you sort through the possible reasons why people might commit suicide.

When you talk about the little things, you may want to include some specific examples from your high school or church.

The line "I didn't really wanna do it" is intense. The deed is done. It's too late for you now. When you finally decide which dress you hope your mom chooses, hold it up for the audience to see.

ugly little insects crawling from my pen. All that pain and anger and loneliness just packed into those frozen little scribbles.

I sat there by myself for a long time, reading and rereading the note, my heart just thumping in my chest. *I'll do it tomorrow,* I thought. *Tomorrow night.* I had a plan. I knew how and I knew when.

It's different reasons for different people, I guess. Loneliness. Depression. Hopelessness. Revenge. Breaking up. Not making the team. Getting rotten grades. Who knows? I don't know. For me, I just didn't see any good reason to keep going. And I thought in some weird, twisted way that by killing myself, I could get back at the people who'd ignored me.

I mean, I know it sounds kinda stupid, but that's how I felt ... *(Pause)*

It's always little things, you know? I mean, like people just not noticing you. Slipping through the cracks or something. Not getting a phone call ...

I'll bet they didn't even realize I was standing there thinking about my note when they turned their backs or made their plans to do stuff together, right there in front of me. Or when they closed up their circle when they saw me coming down the hall.

I'll bet they didn't even realize what I was thinking ... what I was planning. ... *(Pause)*

I didn't really wanna do it. Not really. I didn't really wanna die. No one does. We wanna live. That's the thing — we just want to live. To *live.*

I hope my mom chooses this one. I always loved this dress ... Yeah, that's how I want 'em to remember me. I wonder how many people are gonna show up? I wonder ...

30

Little things.

I wonder sometimes.

I wonder how many other people out there have a note inside 'em, too, just waiting to be scribbled down. Or to be acted out in one desperate moment. I wonder what it would take to delete all those notes, to make 'em all go away forever.

I wonder.

I wonder.

The last thing I remember — when I was lying there and everything was going black ... when the pills finally started working — I heard the phone ring. I wonder who it was ...

Notes for the Actress

Sit back down again.

Let this chilling ending sink in. Freeze as the lights slowly fade to black.

Ideas for the Speaker:

(Before your meeting time, photocopy "Nine Things You Can Do to Help" on page 34. [Photocopy permission is granted for local church use only.]

As JOLENE exits, walk On-stage and face the audience. Then, as the lights come back up, say something like ...)

God cares about you. Right now. This moment. You matter to him. And he wants to give you a second chance. His answer to loneliness is the presence of his Spirit. His answer to emptiness is filling you with himself. His answer to despair is complete forgiveness. He has the answers you need. He has the hope you long for.

Just like the girl in that skit, I wonder sometimes, too ... I wonder how many of us have had those thoughts — how many of us carry around unwritten notes in our heads. I'll bet it's most of us. In fact, I'll bet *every one of us* has thought those thoughts and wondered those things at some point.

(Optional section) You know, even famous Bible heroes got depressed. Elijah reached the point where he gave up on life and just wanted to die (1 Kings 19:1–18). Job was so depressed he wished he'd never been born (Job 3:3–26, 7:15, 10:18, 14:13). Jonah wanted God to kill him when things didn't go his way (Jonah 4). Even Paul talked about his deep desire for the freedom that death brings from the tragedies and pain of this world (Philippians 1:21–24).

It's never God's intention that we take our own lives.

Jesus offers the hope and the peace that we need. He promised us rest and relief from the struggles and despair of this life, *"Come to me, all of you who are weary and carry heavy burdens,"* he said, *"and I will give you rest" (Matthew 11:28)*. That's why Matthew wrote about him, *"He will not crush those who are weak, or quench the smallest hope, until he brings full justice with his final victory. And his name will be the hope of all the world"* (12:20–21).

Does anyone need prayer here today? Right now? *(Pause to pray, if desired.)*

For Further Application:

Suicide is not a peaceful release from life or a romantic escape from suffering into eternal bliss. It's death. And its results can affect families for years and the victim for eternity.

Let's look at some specific things you can do for yourself or someone else if suicidal thoughts start entering your head.

Note to the Speaker:

Understanding suicide and offering help aren't easy. It's a complex issue. Even highly trained counselors don't understand all the motives that lead a person to take his or her own life, nor do they always know what to do about it. However, even if it's tough to talk about, it's important for students to know where to turn and how to help if they see suicidal signs in themselves or in the lives of their friends. There's lots of helpful information on suicide online, but be aware that some sites actually tell kids how to kill themselves rather than offer the counseling they need!

Christian scholars disagree over whether a suicidal person can go to heaven. Some say that suicide is a rejection of salvation in Christ alone and an indication of a lack of saving faith. Others cite examples of people with mental illness or depression who aren't thinking clearly, who make a mistake and pay for it with their lives.

In truth, they're both partially right. Any person, whether killed by suicide or not, who doesn't trust Jesus as his or her personal Savior will suffer punishment and eternal judgment. Only faith in Christ saves. Someone who commits suicide without this saving faith will not go to heaven. On the other hand, sometimes people who are depressed or desperate don't think clearly and they make poor decisions. We shouldn't judge someone by that one single action. God judges us by the condition of our hearts, not by what we've done. (If he did judge by what we've done, none of us would have any hope at all.) Suicide doesn't condemn us, lack of faith does.

Some counselors caution against telling suicidal teens that they will go to hell if they kill themselves. That may be exactly what they think they deserve. They don't need to be threatened, they need to be loved, forgiven, accepted, and embraced. Forgiveness, not suicide, is God's solution to despair.

Verses to Check Out:

- *"I am leaving you with a gift — peace of mind and heart. And the peace I give isn't like the peace the world gives. So don't be troubled or afraid" (John 14:27).*
- *"We are pressed on every side by troubles, but we are not crushed and broken. We are perplexed, but we don't give up and quit. We are hunted down, but God never abandons us. We get knocked down, but we get up again and keep going. Through suffering, these bodies of ours constantly share in the death of Jesus so that the life of Jesus may also be seen in our bodies" (2 Corinthians 4:8–10).*
- *"Don't worry about anything; instead, pray about everything. Tell God what you need, and thank him for all he has done. If you do this, you will experience God's peace, which is far more wonderful than the human mind can understand. His peace will guard your hearts and minds as you live in Christ Jesus" (Philippians 4:6–7).*

Nine Things You Can Do to Help

1. Show an interest in your friend's life. Lots of people equate affection with the amount of attention they receive.
2. Let your friend know that he or she is special and matters to you and to God. Each person on this earth is important. We all matter, but many teens have a low self-image. They think of themselves as worthless. Reasons found in suicide notes often include feelings of failure or worthlessness. Reassure your friend of God's love.
3. Help your friend develop realistic expectations for success, and don't unduly pressure him to succeed. Many teens feel overwhelming stress to perform to the expectations of others, or they have unrealistic expectations for themselves.
4. Don't suggest that someone is stupid, crazy, or weak for considering suicide. Don't mock, argue, debate, or psychoanalyze her. Instead, search with her for a solution and get outside help. Your friend may be calling out to you but doesn't know a better way to ask for help.
5. Show unconditional love and acceptance. Value people regardless of their performance in school or sports. And don't compare one of your friends to the others. Someone will always come up short.
6. Don't be afraid to talk about suicide. It's real and it affects lots of people. You might say, "I've noticed that you seem really sad lately. I know when some people feel desperate or alone, they think about killing themselves. I'm concerned about you. Have you ever had thoughts like that?"
7. Listen. Try to listen without judging or moralizing. Good listeners do not interrupt, change the subject, or wait for a chance to insert their opinion. They listen and try to understand. Period.
8. Keep guns and ammunition inaccessible. Firearms account for two-thirds of all completed youth suicides. Availability of guns only makes it easier for those who are thinking about killing themselves to really carry it out.
9. Pray for your friend.

Not all suicides or attempted suicides have these warning flags. If you fear that someone you know may be suicidal, don't leave him or her alone. Get professional help right away! Most of all, reach out to him or her in love and with understanding. It can make all the difference in the world.

6. Did You Hear about Wendy?

Summary:

Brenda doesn't think she has a problem with gossiping, but has she taken "sharing prayer requests" too far?

Purpose:

Gossiping is a huge problem among teens. Use this drama to reveal the subtle ways we gossip about others. This humorous sketch will (hopefully) also help your students begin looking for ways to build others up instead of tearing them down.

Time:

Four minutes

Props/Set:

Two cell phones (one will be used On-stage, the other will be used Off-stage to call the actress during the monolog)

Topics:

Choices, excuses, gossiping, judging others, prayer, rumors

Cast:

You're Brenda, a sixteen-year-old girl who loves to pass on juicy information about the other people at your church and school. You're peppy and fun, not an airhead, but easily distracted. You genuinely do care about other people, so the possibility that you might actually be gossiping about them has never even crossed your mind. You have a huge crush on Alex.

(You'll also need an Off-stage helper to call Brenda's cell phone during the skit. The director could do this, or you could recruit another member of your youth group to call her.)

Notes:

Before starting this drama, time how long it takes to call Brenda's cell phone from the other one. It may take a few seconds for the connection to go through, and you'll want to make sure Brenda's phone rings at the right times during the drama. If it doesn't ring when it's supposed to, it'll throw off the timing of the piece and create awkward pauses for the actress. Practice calling her during rehearsals to nail down the timing.

Brenda is at a prayer meeting, but don't let this be revealed until the very end of the drama. Tell Brenda to talk really fast, almost hyper, but not to come across as stupid or ditzy. She should be likeable and funny, alternating between the cell phone calls and the rest of her monolog with ease. The trick to pulling off this monolog is to master the pauses in the one-sided phone calls. Encourage your actress to really *hear* the entire conversation. Consider actually talking to her over the phone, as long as it won't distract her.

BRENDA: OK, so I'm next? All right, um, let's see ... Oh! You are *not* gonna believe this. I was talking with Andrea yesterday, and she said that Celeste told her that Kami heard that Alyssa is going out with Alex. I mean *Alex!* Can you believe it?! *(Dreamily)* Wow. He is *so* cute. ... I guess he'd be a good one to start with since he's on the rebound from breaking up with Linda. Ugh! Linda! I can't believe how she treated him! I mean, she totally dumped him after she saw him just *talking* to this other girl, Trish, who works at that ice-cream place in the mall next to The Gap. I mean, the poor guy — *(Cell phone rings)* — oh, just a minute.

Yeah. Yeah. Uh-uh. Whoa. Cool. Uh-huh. No way! Oh, bummer. Totally. OK. Yeah. Whatever. All right. Ga-bye. *(Hangs up the phone.)*

Wrong number. Anyway, where were we? Oh, yeah. Alyssa and Alex, yeah. Hello! What does he see in her, anyway? I mean, she weighs like as much as half the football team. Actually, I'm really concerned about that weight of hers. Maybe we should buy her one of those diet books or something. I mean, my cousin Susanne, who lives in Wichita, lost like 185 pounds in two weeks just by eating celery and olive pits and — *(Cell phone rings)* — oh, just a minute.

Yeah? Cindy! Hey, girlfriend. What's going on? No way! No way! *No way!* Whoa. I can't believe it! Did she really tell you that?! Oh, wow. No, I won't say anything. Of course not. No. I promise. Yeah. Mum's the word. Of course. OK. Love ya. 'Bye. *(Hangs up the phone.)*

You are *not* gonna believe what Cindy just told me! You know that new kid at school?

Notes for the Actress

You're On-stage as the lights come up. Smile, take a big breath, look around, then begin.

You think Alex is the cutest guy at school.

You feel lots of sympathy for poor, dumped Alex.

When you answer the phone, step to the side to have your conversation.

Once again, you get distracted and start talking about other people's problems.

Here you're talking on the phone to your good friend Cindy.

After hanging up the phone, turn to the audience again.

Notes for the Actress

Deliver this whole section (in which you judge his family) in one breath, if possible.

The one with, like, the swoopy _____ *(Insert the name of a popular teen heartthrob)* hair-thing going on? Well, she said — and I don't know if this is true or not, so you have to promise not to tell anyone — OK, promise! OK — anyway, she said his mom just got busted for sneaking drugs out of the clinic where she works as a nurse or something. Can you believe it? Anyway, the kid is probably a drug addict, too. Just like she is. She was probably getting the drugs for him! She'll probably go to jail and he'll be, like, sent to one of those youth homes or something where they don't let you use the phone for, like, twenty-eight days and make you go to group therapy.

Humorously imitate two different voices for this pretend conversation.

"Hello, my name is Bob."

"Hi, Bob."

"My mom's a kleptomaniac."

"That's OK, Bob, we love you anyway. Have a Cheeto."

Poor guy. I bet everyone in his family is an addict — just like that one girl last year, Dana, who got caught shoplifting last — *(Cell phone rings)* — just a sec.

When you finally realize it's the Alex that you like, melt and start poofing your hair.

After you hang up, compose yourself and catch your breath.

Brenda here. Alex? *Alex … Alex! (Get very flustered)* Oh … Um, yeah. I knew it was you. Of course. So, yeah. Friday? … Eight o'clock? … Of course not … I'd die to! I mean, that would be nice. Yeah. *(Optional section)* I gotta go, too. I'm in a prayer meeting at church. *(End of optional section)* OK. 'Bye. *(Hangs up the phone.)*

That was Alex. *Alex … Alex!* He just asked me out on Friday night! Can you believe it? *(Dreamily)* Oh!

(Sighing) So, anyway, me and Alex on Friday … um, Alyssa and her weight … that new

38

kid and his mom ... all those boys at the youth home ... Hmm ... I guess that does it for me. That's all my prayer requests ...

So ... Who's next?

Ideas for the Speaker:

(As BRENDA exits, walk On-stage and face the audience. Then, as the lights come back up, say something like ...)

Most of us don't ever think that we're the ones spreading gossip. It's always someone else. Yet most of us have taken gossiping and talking about people behind their backs to a new level. We're quick to judge, quick to assume, quick to condemn, quick to gossip ... and slow to forgive.

(Optional section) Physical injuries heal. But think about how long it can take to heal a ruined reputation — the person might never recover. And, while it's certainly good to pray for people, we should never use that as an excuse for sharing juicy tidbits of gossip or passing on the latest rumors.

No wonder James writes, *"People can tame all kinds of animals and birds and reptiles and fish, but no one can tame the tongue. It is an uncontrollable evil, full of deadly poison"* (James 3:7–8).

Poison. That's what drips off some people's tongues.

Think of times when you've seen someone get hurt by the poison of another person's words. It might be a friend. Or a parent. Or a brother or a sister. Odds are, if you're honest, there have been times when you've been poisoned. And I'll bet there have been times when you've done the poisoning. We wound. We poison. And we're wounded in return — all by the power of careless words.

Words can help or hurt. They can heal or scar. Think carefully about the words you're using. Are you poisoning someone's reputation? Or are you healing it? Let's go to Jesus right now and ask him to help us heal and restore rather than wound and destroy by the words we use ... Because the antidote we need — the only one that'll ever truly help us — is Jesus.

Verses to Check Out:

- *"A gossip goes around revealing secrets, but those who are trustworthy can keep a confidence"* (Proverbs 11:13).
- *"A gossip tells secrets, so don't hang around with someone who talks too much"* (Proverbs 20:19).
- *"So also, the tongue is a small thing, but what enormous damage it can do. A tiny spark can set a great forest on fire"* (James 3:5, see also the context by reading James 3:1–12).
- *"But I tell you that every careless word that people speak, they shall give an accounting for it in the day of judgment"* (Matthew 12:36, NASB).

7. Stepping over the Line

Summary:

After watching a surprising turn of events in a college basketball game, Jose has started thinking about how integrity and sports mix. However, he's not sure if he's ready to live with that much honesty.

Purpose:

Use this drama to ask the question, "What does it mean to cheat?" Most students would agree that it's wrong to cheat. It's just that we don't all agree on what cheating and dishonesty actually are. This drama will help bring some of those tough issues to the surface.

Time:

Three to four minutes

Props/Set:

A basketball, basketball shoes, and an outfit of someone who's going to play a pick-up game of basketball (shorts and a T-shirt)

Topics:

Cheating, choices, excuses, honesty, integrity, little things, lying, sports, winning

Cast:

You're Jose, a sixteen-year-old guy who loves to watch college basketball. You don't usually think of breaking the rules of the game as "cheating," just a missed call by the ref, but now you're starting to wonder how far a life of integrity really goes.

Notes:

If your actor knows any basketball tricks, such as spinning a basketball on his finger, he could intersperse them throughout this monolog. When you're casting someone for this part, consider choosing a student who is known to be an athlete. It'll add credibility to his character when he talks about basketball. Have him pull on his basketball shoes and then lace and tie them during the monolog as if he's getting ready to head out to the court for a pick-up game.

41

Notes for the Actor

If it's not basketball season, you can say you saw the game last year instead of last night. Feel free to insert the names of other popular college basketball teams in your region that might play each other.

You know your stuff. You're a big hoops fan.

Reenact these events with enthusiasm. You're still surprised by how it all played out.

JOSE: So, I'm watching this hoops game on TV the other night. Duke versus Georgia Tech. And Duke was down by three, and this sophomore — Mohammed Abdul Rahaji — hits a fade-away three-pointer at the buzzer to tie the game and send it into overtime. I'm like, "Ye-e-e-a-a-ah!"

So that's all good, 'cause I'm a Duke fan …

But here's the thing. The ref called it a three, right? But Mohammed goes up to the ref and tells him his foot was on the line! And they look at the instant replay and you could see that he was right. It was only a two, and of course in NCAA Division One hoops, a ref can check a courtside monitor to determine if a shot attempt was a two-pointer or a three-pointer. So he did. And he *changed his call.* The ref calls it a two-pointer and Duke loses the game.

So then the crowd goes nuts. They totally boo this guy. And his coach goes ballistic on him. He gets right in his face, on national TV, and I'm thinking, "He's gonna punch his lights out!" But he just screams at him, you know, like coaches do, and Mohammed is cool about the whole thing. Doesn't even blink.

And one of the on-air sports announcers says something like, "If the ref makes a call in your favor, you *never* correct him! That young man just lost his team this game!"

It was crazy.

And at the press conference after the game, they interviewed Mohammed Abdul Rahaji and he says, "My foot was on the line. I knew it. I had to say something or I wouldn't-a been able to sleep tonight." And then he says this: "I'm a Muslim. To us, honesty is more important than winning." And then he walks off and they cut to a commercial!

Whoa.

So that's when I started thinking about it, you know — what would I have done?

I know I'd tell the ref if he called something that *didn't* go my way. Everyone would. Coaches and players do that all the time — complaining about calls and stuff. The crowd does, too. But they booed this guy for being honest.

They booed him.

Maybe you're only supposed to be honest about something when it ends up being good for you. Maybe that's the deal ...

I'd never really thought of it as a matter of *honesty*. I mean, c'mon! It's just a game, right? If the ref doesn't see something, it's OK ... it's not wrong unless you get caught, right?

So he says, "I'm a Muslim. ... To us, honesty is more important than winning."

And I'm thinking, "Well, hey there, buddy, I'm a Christian, and honesty is more important to us than winning, too!"

But then again, I wouldn't have said anything to that ref. I woulda just been thankful he didn't see my foot go over the line ...

I think to most people winning *is* more important than being honest. Otherwise, they wouldn't have booed him; they woulda given him a standing ovation.

Huh.

I never really thought about that before.

Notes for the Actor

Here you're starting to wonder: How does my faith affect my life? What difference does it make at home? At school? At work? On the basketball court?

You used to think that these things were true, but you're not so convinced anymore.

You wish your faith would have changed how you might have responded, but it probably wouldn't have.

When you're finished, walk Off-stage with your basketball as the lights slowly fade.

Ideas for the Speaker:

(You could lead this discussion in a number of directions. You could address the issues of morally upstanding people from other religions, or you could direct students to examine and apply honesty and integrity to their own lives and reevaluate their priorities when it comes to sports and life. As JOSE exits, walk On-stage and face the audience. Then, as the lights come back up, say something like ...)

What's more important, winning or honesty? Getting a good grade, or avoiding cheating at all costs? Saving a little time by copying someone else's report, or doing what's right?

Integrity isn't something you can turn on and off whenever you feel like it. Integrity cares more about what's right than about what's convenient. And a person with integrity will stand with his head held high even when the rest of the world boos him.

Let's admit it. It's pretty easy to get away with stuff today. You can just go online and pull up an essay on any subject you need. Just download it, print it out, and you're done. It's easy to break the speed limit. Most people do it all the time. In fact, if you want to, you can cut corners and cheat in almost every area of your life. Work. School. Tests. Relationships. Taxes. People do it all the time. And what does God think? Well, that's the kicker. *"The LORD hates cheating, but he delights in honesty"* (Proverbs 11:1).

How much of your life would change if you decided to be *completely* honest? To live with total integrity? What kind of a life would that be?

Well, it'd be a Christian one.

So, here's the real question: What's more important in your life — your goals or God's? Your plans or his? Getting ahead or following Jesus, wherever that might lead?

It's time we asked ourselves how far we're willing to go in living out our faith. *(Break into discussion groups or end with prayer.)*

Verses to Check Out:

- "Yes, what joy for those whose record the LORD has cleared of sin, whose lives are lived in complete honesty!" *(Psalm 32:2).*
- "Nothing evil will be allowed to enter [heaven] — no one who practices shameful idolatry and dishonesty — but only those whose names are written in the Lamb's Book of Life" *(Revelation 21:27).*
- "But as for your question, you know the commandments: 'Do not murder. Do not commit adultery. Do not steal. Do not testify falsely. Do not cheat. Honor your father and mother'" *(Mark 10:19).*

8. Valley of the Shadow

Summary:

In the aftermath of a freak traffic accident, Nate is struggling with accepting the death of his younger brother. At last, through his faith, he begins to see things from a more eternal perspective.

Purpose:

Use this drama to explore the gut-wrenching reality of death and point to a lasting hope that comes from true faith in Christ.

Time:

Seven to eight minutes (This is the longest monolog in the book.)

Props/Set:

A chair, table, or desk; calculus textbooks; papers; pencils; calculator

Topics:

Anger, conversion, death, emptiness, faith, family relationships, grief, hope, Jesus, pain, questioning God, suffering

Cast:

You're Nate, an eighteen-year-old guy who's having a hard time understanding how your sixth-grade brother, Tommy, could really be dead. For a long time after you heard the news, you didn't cry. But now, at last, you realize the truth that your brother is with Christ in heaven and that it's OK to cry and be honest about your feelings of loss and grief. Sometimes it takes more guts to cry than it does to stuff your feelings down deep and pretend that it doesn't hurt.

As the sketch begins, you're trying to cram for a calculus exam, but you can't concentrate.

All of us have friends or relatives who have died. Death is the bad-news result of sin: *"For the wages of sin is death"* (Romans 6:23a). That's bad news, all right. But the good news comes in the second part of the same

Bible verse: *"but the free gift of God is eternal life through Christ Jesus our Lord" (Romans 6:23b).* In this monolog, you realize the painful reality of the first part of this verse and the lasting comfort of the second part.

Notes:

As one of the longest monologs in this collection, this drama will take some work. Make sure your actor puts in the time needed to do it right. The images of light and darkness serve to highlight life and death.

The blocking in this sketch grows out of Nate's tour of the sites in his narrative (including the principal's office, the funeral home, and Tommy's bedroom) and his interaction with his calculus work.

Notes for the Actor

You're On-stage trying to study for your calc test. You're trying to concentrate but you can't.

Gesture to where Mr. Weathers had you sit.

Pause here and go back to your work for a moment.

Visualize Tommy, your twelve-year-old little brother, lying there, dead in the casket, as you explain this section.

Go to a new position On-stage and look into the imaginary casket as you begin to deliver this intense section.

Try to see each of these specific memories as you talk about them.

You really miss your brother.

NATE: Guys aren't supposed to cry. That's what they say. It's not cool. Not tough.

So I didn't cry. Not when they took me out of my third-hour English lit. class. Not when our principal, Mr. Weathers, led me to his office, motioned to a chair, and told me to "Have a seat." Yeah, I knew something had happened. Something bad. But I didn't show it. I just sat there in his slick, black leather chair and waited.

And then my mom walked in with a police officer and I saw the look in her eyes, and I knew. But I didn't cry. Not even when they told me the news. Even when mom started shaking. Not even then ...

I almost cried at the funeral, staring at Tommy lying there cold and unmoving in the casket that was too big for him. He was only in the sixth grade.

But I didn't cry. Because guys don't cry.

So after the funeral, a lot of old people I didn't know came up to me and shook my hand and told me how brave I was.

And I just kinda nodded and acted polite.

Then, when it was all over, I went back to look at his body one last time.

There's something about seeing your little brother in a coffin. The same guy you used to joke around with and make fun of and pick on and laugh with. You start to remember stuff. Weird stuff. Like ... last winter when I took him snowboarding for the first time ... or water-skiing at the lake by Uncle Howie's cabin ... going out for pizza with him on his tenth birthday ... the time he didn't make the soccer team and I met him at the mall and we played video games together so long that Mom got worried and came looking for us ... that day when I was a freshman and we were wrestling around in the living room and I ended up getting mad and punching him in the neck and we had to go the emergency room because he was having trouble breathing ... how scared I was ... how empty I felt ... how much I loved him ...

Two years ago, when we picked him up from church camp, he was so proud! He showed me his Bible. On the front page his counselor had written down a date and circled it. "July 24th, 200__ *(Insert the date for two years ago)*, Tommy's spiritual birthday!" it said. Tommy grinned and told me, "On Wednesday, when I trusted in Jesus, God and all the angels started this party — you know — up in heaven. And someday I get to join 'em!"

I guess he was right ...

So then, Mom tells me it's time to go. Everyone else has left. So I take one last look around and then follow her to the car. When we get back to the apartment, I change out of my church clothes and put on jeans and a T-shirt again. It's almost like nothing has happened.

Then I walk past his door. I half expect him to run out and laugh at me for being so stupid to believe that he could actually be dead. When he's really alive ... alive ... alive ...

But, of course, no one comes. The door stays shut.

I tilt my head and look at it, and then glance down the hallway. Silence. Nobody. So then I'm nervous.

I reach out and turn the knob.

The door swings open and I'm looking at his room. Late afternoon sunlight filters through the curtains. A thin cloud of dust seems to

Notes for the Actor

Leave the casket for a moment and take us to the day Tommy came home from camp.

You're angry that he was right — that he's dead.

Move to a new position On-stage. Now, you're home.

Act out this section as you talk about it.

Notes for the Actor

Direct the attention of the audience to your little brother's room. Give us a tour. Show us, by where you look and gesture, where everything would be On-stage.

Go to your desk and look at your homework.

Page through your books.

Your bitterness at the whole situation is seeping through again.

Face the audience and stop looking around his room when you describe the car accident.

Nothing makes sense anymore. You're angry at God for the brutal and senseless string of events that ended your brother's life.

hang in the air. The room is thick with shadows. I step inside and let the door close behind me.

The first thing I see is his bed, neatly made. Too neat. Mom must have made it this morning. Everything else is the same. His walls are covered with posters of hoops players and concert shots of his favorite bands. His dresser drawer is half open and a sock hangs over the edge. Limp. Dead.

There's a pile of books on his desk. Even his pre-algebra homework that I was helping him with is still laying out. And that gets me thinking about how I have a calculus test coming up and how I'll probably bomb it, even though I'm usually pretty good at calc. When you know all the right symbols and formulas, all you gotta do is plug in the numbers and it all comes together. It all works out. It all makes sense.

Unlike life. *(Slam the calculus book shut.)*

It was a car accident. That's what killed him. He was running out into the road to get a playground ball during recess, and this guy who was too busy talking on his cell phone to notice that he was about to kill my brother ran the red light. Maybe if Tommy would have died rescuing a drowning baby or something, it would make more sense. But it was just a stupid traffic accident!

Outside, someone's dog barks. I look up for a moment and then back to his desk. There's his GameBoy. A bunch of CDs. His Bible.

I pick it up.

At the funeral, the preacher said that God is as sad about death as we are. At first I'm thinking, *Yeah, right! He's the one who took my brother away!* But then the guy talked about how Jesus cried when his friend, Lazarus, died. That was kind of a shock to me. Jesus cried?

So I open it to the first page.

I mean, he was pretty tough. Carpenters aren't wimps. And Jesus spent nearly six weeks in the desert without a bite to eat. He had a face-off with the devil and didn't even blink. He took on a whole mob of crooks and drove 'em out of the temple. And then the beatings and torture and crucifixion ... None of that stuff made him cry. None of it.

But he cried when his friend died. His heart broke. It hurt so much he didn't know what else to do. Even though his friend was a believer. Even though Jesus knew he'd see him in heaven. Even with all that hope. He still cried. And the people who saw it said, "Wow. Look how much he loved his friend!"

Huh. Maybe Jesus *can* understand.

So there's the date of Tommy's birthday. I pick up a blue pen with a baseball logo on it and scribble next to it: "September, 18th, 200__ *(Insert the current year)* Tommy joins the party."

"See, ya, Tommy," I whisper, as the tears begin to fall. "I'm gonna miss you. I love you. Save a seat for me at the party."

And before I leave, I walk over and raise the blinds so his room isn't so full of shadows anymore.

Notes for the Actor

As you discover these realizations about the personality of Jesus and the depth of his love, your anger and bitterness begin to melt away. Jesus is the answer. You know that now. Before you knew it in your head. Now you know it in your heart.

You don't want to get preachy here, you just want to summarize the Bible story.

This drama ends on a note of hope, as does the life of everyone who believes in Christ.

Freeze. Fadeout.

Ideas for the Speaker:

(As NATE exits, walk On-stage and face the audience. Then, as the lights come back up, say something like ...)

Death stalks us all. It picks us off one by one. But with Christ, we can have a hope that reaches beyond the grave and a confidence that even death cannot shake (see Hebrews 6:19).

The name of this monolog — "Valley of the Shadow" — comes from Psalm 23:4 (NIV), *"Even though I walk through the valley of the shadow of death, I will fear no evil, for you are with me; your rod and your staff, they comfort me."* All of us walk through the dark valley of death's shadow, but we need not fear, not when we have Jesus to walk with us and to comfort us.

Let's split into small groups and take some time to pray. Let's focus our prayers in three directions. You may need to pray for unbelieving friends and family members. That's direction number one. Pray that they would be reborn spiritually. Or you may need to pray for people you know who are grieving over the loss of a loved one. That's option number two. The third choice is to pray for a greater confidence in the promises and love of God. Sometimes doubt overwhelms us in this fallen, dying world, and we need to simply rely on the promises of God and let ourselves rest in his waiting arms. Let's get into groups of three to four people and take these requests to the God who walks with us and comforts us with his presence, power, and love.

Verses to Check Out:

- *"And now, brothers and sisters, I want you to know what will happen to the Christians who have died so you will not be full of sorrow like people who have no hope. For since we believe that Jesus died and was raised to life again, we also believe that when Jesus comes, God will bring back with Jesus all the Christians who have died"* (1 Thessalonians 4:13–14).
- *"Everyone dies because all of us are related to Adam, the first man. But all who are related to Christ, the other man, will be given new life"* (1 Corinthians 15:22).
- *"Can anything ever separate us from Christ's love? Does it mean he no longer loves us if we have trouble or calamity, or are persecuted, or are hungry or cold or in danger or threatened with death? (Even the Scriptures say, 'For your sake we are killed every day; we are being slaughtered like sheep.') No, despite all these things, overwhelming victory is ours through Christ, who loved us"* (Romans 8:35–37).

9. Licking the Fence

Summary:

Adrian has never been one to listen to advice. Instead, he has always learned things the hard way. But now his choices have caught up with him and affected more people than just himself.

Purpose:

Teens don't typically think through the consequences of their choices. They don't consider what might go wrong or who they might hurt. This drama will remind your students that all of our choices affect other people and that we need to think about the unintended consequences of our decisions.

Time:

Six to seven minutes

Props/Set:

A wheelchair

Topics:

Addictions, choices, consequences, drinking, drugs, guilt, life, maturity, obedience, regrets, temptation, traps, warnings

Cast:

You're Adrian, a sixteen-year-old guy who caused a drunk driving accident. You're the kind of guy who doesn't really listen to other people's advice, and this time it cost you, big time. A nine-year-old girl was killed. The more you think about the accident, the more you're filled with guilt, regret, and remorse. Don't be afraid to get emotionally involved in this drama. It's pretty powerful.

Notes:

From the moment Adrian wheels himself On-stage in the wheelchair, the audience will know something serious has happened. Encourage your actor to tell the opening story about licking the fence in a lighthearted way. The stuff at the end is really serious.

When you *choose* to do something, the consequences of your choice cease to be an accident. Often teens don't think much about the consequences of their choices. This drama will help them see that everything we do affects other people.

(Roll On-stage in a wheelchair. Face the audience and then begin.)

ADRIAN: I used to skip rocks at my uncle's cabin on the lake all the time when I was a kid. You get these flat stones and throw 'em kinda sidearm and if you nail it just right, you can get maybe seven or eight skips out of each one ... Bam. Bam. Bam. Bam-bam-bam-bam ... Before they sink to the bottom ... Before they disappear below the surface.

(Sigh) I admit it. I was one of those kids who licked the metal fence when I was in the third grade. I never would've done it in the summer or anything. I wouldn't have even *thought* about doing it in the wintertime ... except some kid told me what would happen if I did. He said my tongue would get stuck to the frozen metal and I would have to rip off the top layer of tongue skin just to get free. He told me how stupid it was to lick a fence in the wintertime. So, ten minutes later, what do I do? I go outside for recess and I stick my tongue against the frozen metal fence.

And what can I say? My tongue got stuck, and I had to rip off the top layer of tongue skin to get free, just like that kid had said. And, um ... well ... lemme tell ya, blood got all over, gushing outta my mouth. I run into the school yelling, "Heh! Heh! I'm beeding! I'm beeding!" — it's pretty hard to talk when half your tongue is hanging from a fence outside.

And my teacher fainted. She hit her head on the desk and had to be taken to the hospital. And I had to eat Jell-O for a month.

(Proudly) When I lick a fence, *I lick a fence ...*

It was like being told what not to do made me want to do it all the more! Yeah,

---

Notes for the Actor

Let the words about sinking below the surface hang in the air for a moment before continuing.

Smile and tell the story of licking the fence in a lighthearted way. The rest of the drama is really serious. Let this section be funny.

Yell, "Help! Help! I'm bleeding!" with your mouth open.

You would have never admitted this before. But you've done a lot of thinking over the last year or two.

Notes for the Actor

Instead of ecstasy, you may wish to insert the name of another popular party drug in your part of the country. Then, let the words "last year" hang in the air.

Say these lines about the ripples chasing each other thoughtfully, but don't get "preachy."

When you say "I do my own thing," you're not justifying yourself, you're simply describing yourself.

Really see the accident as you describe it. It's still vivid in your mind, even after all this time, but it's hard to talk about.

sometimes I think if stupidity were a drug, I'd be high all the time.

I've never been one to learn things the easy way.

So then, when I got a little older, in junior high *(Or middle school)*, it was smoking.

Then as a freshman, it was drugs ... Ecstasy, mostly.

And then, last year ... *(Look at the wheelchair)*

Well ... you know, after it happened, I spent a lot of time thinking. There wasn't much else to do in the hospital except think. And whenever I thought about the girl, I remembered my sister that summer at my uncle's cabin, 'cause they were about the same age ...

I remembered skipping those rocks and everything. 'Cause one thing I used to watch were the ripples. You can't drop a rock in a lake without sending out ripples. They go in every direction, all the way to the shore. You can't really help it. It's just the way it is ... One ripple after the other. Chasing each other back to the shore ...

So, anyway, everyone tried to warn me about drinking. But I do my own thing, you know? I've always been that way. Hard-headed. Stubborn. I gotta put my hand on the burner to see if it's hot ...

So ... that night ... it'd been raining. The pavement was wet. I remember that. 'Cause all the lights from the ambulances and cop cars were flashing, reflecting off the road. I remember broken glass. All over. And I was lying on a stretcher. Rain was getting in my eyes, so I turned my head ... and I saw her arm. The little girl's arm. Hanging out of the car.

It was soaked in blood.

This lady — her mom — was screaming. Over and over. She wouldn't stop. They couldn't calm her down.

I remember telling 'em it was an accident.

Then she saw me. She came running over.

"I'm sorry ... " I said. I was crying by then, too. "It was an accident."

"No!" she yelled. She was shaking. "*You* made the choice. *You* got behind the wheel. You started the car. You drove it. You hit us. *You made the choice!* It's not an accident!"

Then they took her away. She was crying so hard they had to help her stand up.

Later on, they told me her daughter woulda been ten in a week. The same age my sister was that summer. At my uncle's cabin. When we used to skip the rocks ...

I said I was sorry. And I was ... but sorry's not enough. She's gone ... and it wasn't an accident.

When I was in the hospital, all I could think of was watching those rocks skip across the lake and then sink from view. And those ripples. One after the other. Chasing each other back to shore ... And the girl's arm that night — limp and still and bloody.

It wasn't an accident. It was cause and effect.

Because when you choose to do something, the consequences cease to be an accident. Ripples. All the way to shore.

Oh, God. What have I done? *(After you've delivered your last line, freeze as the lights slowly fade to black.)*

Notes for the Actor

Let your pace quicken as you retell the account of talking with the girl's mother. Show the urgency and desperation in her voice.

You really are sorry. But you can't undo it. You chose to drink that night. And now a little girl is dead. Pause as you realize that it wasn't really an accident.

You're not using God's name in vain here, you're uttering a desperate, gut-level prayer.

57

Ideas for the Speaker:

(You could emphasize drinking or drug use in your discussion, or, you could draw out a broader application about choices and consequences. The ideas below refer to choices in general rather than to drinking, specifically.

After the lights have faded and ADRIAN has exited, walk On-stage and face the audience. Then, as the lights come back up, say something like …)

We're all an awful lot like the kid in that monolog. Too often we know what the right thing or the smart thing is to do, but we don't do it. And every choice we make is a rock. Every one of 'em sends another bunch of waves rippling through the lives of other people.

Like the kid said, "When you choose to do something, the consequences cease to be an accident." We can't participate in a series of choices and then claim that the result wasn't our fault or was an "accident." Sure, the results may have been unintended, but that doesn't excuse us from being responsible for causing them.

And just like this kid, when we hear about something we know is wrong, we're drawn to it all the more; at least, part of us is pulled toward it, toward sin. We still have those evil desires inside of us. All of us do: *"Temptation comes from the lure of our own evil desires. These evil desires lead to evil actions, and evil actions lead to death"* (James 1:14–15).

As Paul wrote in Romans 7:24–25, *"Oh, what a miserable person I am! Who will free me from this life that is dominated by sin? Thank God! The answer is in Jesus Christ our Lord. So you see how it is: In my mind I really want to obey God's law, but because of my sinful nature I am a slave to sin."*

It doesn't do any good to just feel bad about something in the past. But if you're willing to let God use the sorrow for your wrong choices to change your attitude, it can lead you to repentance. *"For God can use sorrow in our lives to help us turn away from sin and seek salvation. We will never regret that kind of sorrow. But sorrow without repentance is the kind that results in death"* (2 Corinthians 7:10).

What fences have you been enticed to lick? What dark roads have you been lured to walk? What do you need to tell God about or change right now? *(End with prayer.)*

58

Verses to Check Out:

- "These are the proverbs of Solomon, David's son, king of Israel. The purpose of these proverbs is to teach people wisdom and discipline, and to help them understand wise sayings. Through these proverbs, people will receive instruction in discipline, good conduct, and doing what is right, just, and fair. These proverbs will make the simpleminded clever. They will give knowledge and purpose to young people" (Proverbs 1:1–4).
- "For the grace of God that brings salvation has appeared to all men. It teaches us to say 'No' to ungodliness and worldly passions, and to live self-controlled, upright and godly lives in this present age" (Titus 2:11–12, NIV).
- "So think clearly and exercise self-control. Look forward to the special blessings that will come to you at the return of Jesus Christ. Obey God because you are his children. Don't slip back into your old ways of doing evil; you didn't know any better then" (1 Peter 1:13–14).

10. The Real Thing

Summary:

When a friend from Brian's past asks him about his faith journey, he's forced to admit that he hasn't been living for Jesus at all; he's only been living for himself.

Purpose:

Use this drama to convict nominal Christians of complacency and compromise.

Time:

Five to six minutes

Props/Set:

A cash register; a suit or uniform for a fancy restaurant; money in different denominations; a table, desk, or countertop on which to play with it

Topics:

Appearances, authenticity, choices, compromise, conviction, counterfeit spirituality, faith, fitting in, popularity

Cast:

You're Brian, a seventeen-year-old guy. You work at an expensive restaurant and you like to go snowboarding on the weekends with your friends from school. You committed your life to Christ about two years ago, but now you realize you haven't been living for Jesus at all. You're faced with a question: "What am I gonna do about it?"

Notes:

Brian should dress like someone who might be working the cash register at an upscale restaurant. He's not stuck-up, he simply has a job that requires lots of trust. Whenever he pauses in the monolog, he can count money, stack it, or sort it into piles. Use real money rather than fake money. (If you were to use pretend money, it would undermine the message of authenticity that's so central to this drama.)

BRIAN: I guess I've been here, oh, 'bout seven or eight months now. Something like that.

We get lots of money through here at Angelo's. Sometimes ten or fifteen thou a day. It was listed in some magazine as one of the Top One Hundred Steak Restaurants in North America ...

And when you start working the cash register, Mr. Angelo goes through this whole thing about how to find counterfeit money.

"Look for differences," he says, "not similarities."

You see, the deal is, you compare the bill you're not sure about with the real thing. You hold 'em up next to each other and then you check out the face to see how lifelike it is — you look at the spacing of the serial numbers, the colors along the edges of the bill ... everything.

Like Mr. Angelo says, "You can always tell a counterfeit when you look close enough."

Well, yesterday I found my first counterfeit bill. I mean, I've been working the cash register since I started, and you get to know money pretty well. So, I'm suspicious of this bill and it turns out I was right. The picture gave it away. It wasn't quite right.

It was pretty cool. I turned it in to Mr. Angelo. I'll probably get a raise or something. Maybe get recruited by the Secret Service ... Work in the counterfeit money division ... That'd be cool. *(Pause)*

So, last weekend I'm meeting some friends at the White Mountain Ski Resort, right? Jake and Aaron. From school. You know, to go snowboarding.

And I'm standing there at the check-in area at the Chalet looking for 'em, when I see her.

Notes for the Actor

As you begin this monolog, you're counting the money from a cash register.

When you talk on behalf of your boss, you're not mocking him, just imitating him.

Hold up some money as you offhandedly list these ways of discovering counterfeit money.

Don't give too much away here. You're simply foreshadowing.

As you transition into the ski resort story, the audience won't see any connection yet. But don't worry, they'll get it by the end of the monolog.

Notes for the Actor

If you wish, replace "Colorado Springs" with the name of another city to which people from your area might move.

By saying this run-on sentence in one breath, you can bring more emphasis and impact to Sierra's question.

When you ask these questions, imitate her voice, but don't mock her.

You're ashamed that you haven't been living for Jesus like you should've been.

At first, I couldn't believe it was really her. I mean, I hadn't seen her in like two years — ever since she moved to Colorado Springs.

But it was her. Sierra. There was no mistaking her laugh or the way she flipped her hair to the side. It was her.

She runs up and we're all, like, hugging and saying "Hi" and everything. I liked the hugging part …

And she tells me how she misses our school but that she's found a bunch of new friends and things were good and her dad loves his new job and she baby-sits for this guy who's a writer and she's found this awesome church and everything, and then she says it.

"So, how's your walk going?" That's what she asked me.

And I'm like, "My walk? What are you talking about?"

"You know. Your walk with Jesus. How's it going?"

And I just stood there for a minute and let the question sink in. *How was my walk with Jesus?* I kinda kicked it around in my head and I finally said something like, "Oh, good … good, you know. Just taking it one day at a time — " And she just smiled and nodded and didn't seem to read between the lines.

So then my friends show up and she has to go meet up with her group anyway. And that was it. We exchanged e-mail addresses and said we'd write and then she was gone, swallowed up in the crowd of skiers and snowboarders …

Man, why did she have to go and ask me about that? I hadn't seen her in two years and then she just blurts out, "How's your walk with Jesus going?"

I mean, she was the one who invited me on the retreat in the first place — back when I was a sophomore. That retreat when I made a commitment. When I said I was gonna live for Jesus from then on ...

I just stood there thinking about how the Brian she knew then and the Brian I am now are, like, two totally different people. The music I listen to is different. The friends I hang out with are different. The stuff I do on the weekends ... the words I use ... the T-shirts I wear — all different. Way different.

Things changed. Slowly, you know. Not all at once. It was like a series of little choices that all seemed pretty much OK until finally I became embarrassed about the things I used to be proud of and proud of the things I used to be embarrassed about ... And I was saying "yes" to things I'd never have said "yes" to back then. When I was close to Sierra.

When I was close to Jesus.

So I followed my friends like a zombie through the lobby to the place where you buy your lift tickets. But I wasn't thinking about snowboarding at all. I was thinking about her question, "So, how's your walk going?" I hadn't told her the truth. Not by a long shot. *(Pause)*

I found my first counterfeit bill yesterday. You can always tell a fake when you look close enough. You can always see if it's genuine or not.

Huh. Yeah. No kidding.

Notes for the Actor

You're finally realizing that you've been living a counterfeit life.

No one *falls* into sin, complacency, or compromise. We *drift* into it. Slowly. One choice at a time. That's what has been happening to you.

As you begin this last paragraph, pick up a twenty and stare at it.

Let that last line hang in the air as you turn and exit and the lights fade to black.

Ideas for the Speaker:

(As BRIAN exits, walk On-stage and face the audience. Then, as the lights come back up, say something like …)

Some people are so good at pretending they're believers that they've even convinced themselves. But according to Jesus, if you don't put your faith into practice, if you don't live it out, if your life doesn't change because of your relationship with him, you're not a believer. You're a fraud. A counterfeit.

Once, when he was talking about false prophets, he said that you can always identify them by the fruit of their lives. Fruit can't be faked. Listen to what he said.

> *"A good tree can't produce bad fruit, and a bad tree can't produce good fruit. So every tree that does not produce good fruit is chopped down and thrown into the fire. Yes, the way to identify a tree or a person is by the kind of fruit that is produced. Not all people who sound religious are really godly. They may refer to me as 'Lord,' but they still won't enter the Kingdom of Heaven. The decisive issue is whether they obey my Father in heaven"* (Matthew 7:18–21).

Jesus said those words right before telling that famous story of his about the two people building their houses — you know, how the one guy built his house on the rock and the other guy built on sand. Jesus said that the man who puts God's word into practice is like the wise man building on the rock. But the one who hears his words and doesn't put them into practice is like the guy who builds on sand. One day his house — his life — is gonna crumble.

Right now, take a close look at your heart and your life. Compare your Christian walk to the real thing — a person who puts Jesus' words into practice. Look closely. Look for differences, not similarities. Have you been living a counterfeit life?

If so, what are you gonna do about it? What do you need to tell God right now? He's waiting. His grace is available. His arms are open. Tell him what you need to. Do what you have to. Let's pray …

Notes for the Leader:

Some Christians believe that once you decide to be a Christian, you can't lose your salvation. Others believe that you can. Both groups acknowledge that all too often those who say that they're believers don't live the lifestyle of a true Christian. The first group of believers might say that those who are living ungodly lives are "backsliding" or were never truly a Christian in the first place. The second group might say those people have rejected Christ and lost their salvation. In either case, the person needs to repent and turn to Christ. Whatever your theological orientation, emphasize that nominal Christians need to make a change *today* and trust Christ for forgiveness *right now*, rather than getting sidetracked from repentance by wondering whether or not they were ever true Christians in the first place.

Verses to Check Out:

- *"If the godly compromise with the wicked, it is like polluting a fountain or muddying a spring" (Proverbs 25:26).*
- *"If a person is ashamed of me and my message, I, the Son of Man, will be ashamed of that person when I return in my glory and in the glory of the Father and the holy angels" (Luke 9:26).*
- *"Teach me your way, O LORD , and I will walk in your truth; give me an undivided heart, that I may fear your name" (Psalm 86:11, NIV).*
- *"You hypocrites! Isaiah was prophesying about you when he said, 'These people honor me with their lips, but their hearts are far away. Their worship is a farce, for they replace God's commands with their own man-made teachings' " (Matthew 15:7–9).*

11. Reflections

Summary:

Bridget and her boyfriend went too far, and now she's haunted by the choices she made and the things he did with her ... and to her.

Purpose:

Many teens struggle with regrets from going too far physically. The guilt can be crushing. This drama will bring these feelings to the surface and help you deal openly with them. You could also use this monolog to introduce the topic of date rape.

Time:

Four to five minutes

Props/Set:

A dresser with a mirror and a chair

Topics:

Anger, belonging, brokenness, choices, compromise, consequences, date rape, regrets, relationships, scars, second chances, sex, temptation

Cast:

You're Bridget, a fifteen-year-old girl who's reeling in the aftermath of a relationship that went too far physically. You didn't stop when you should have, and now you don't know what to do to get rid of your feelings of guilt. Four months ago your boyfriend took advantage of you, and you let him do things that you still regret. Every time you look in the mirror, you're reminded of your painful past.

Notes:

Bridget could deliver sections of this monolog with her back partially to the audience and her head tilted to the side so that the audience only sees her profile. Position the mirror so that the audience can see Bridget's reflection. You may wish to use a mirror with a long crack in it.

The script bounces back and forth from Bridget's past to her present, from her struggles to her regrets. Encourage your actress to savor the pauses and transitions and to use them to add to the disconnected, shattered mood of this piece.

Notes for the Actress

You're seated On-stage combing your hair when the lights come up and the drama begins.

Don't sing the words, just choose a rhythm that you can use whenever you repeat them.

Change your posture as you shift gears and begin telling your personal story.

Change your inflection whenever you shift to the words of the country song, then pick up again where you left off in your story.

BRIDGET: There's this song. You know, this country song. I used to listen to it back when we lived in Kentucky.

What do you see when you look in the mirror?
What do you see in your eyes and your face?
I see the past like a tower before me.
Oh, who has the keys ... the keys, to this place?

I knew we were pushing the boundaries. I knew it, but I didn't do anything about it. I mean, he was the first guy I'd ever really gone out with ... the first guy to ever tell me he cared about me ... the first guy to ever touch me that way.

I was fourteen, he was a couple years older. It was summer. He was visiting relatives.

I don't know, I mean, I never asked him, but I think he'd been with other girls before.

He told me it'd be all right. *(Pause)*

He told me it'd bring us closer. He said I could show him that I really loved him. I thought that once school started, the pain would just go away ... But it hasn't.

What do you see when you look in the mirror?
What do you see in your eyes and your face?

He could tell I didn't really wanna go there — you know, go any further. I mean, sure, part of me did. Of course. I'm not saying it wasn't *partly* my fault. I'm not saying that. I'm just saying ... he didn't stop.

"No," I said. "Not tonight." We'd done it before, but I didn't wanna do it again.

I see the past like a tower before me.

Oh, who has the keys ... the keys, to this place?

"Come on," he said. He was breathing fast. His breath felt hot and angry on my cheek.

"Please. I wanna stop," I said.

At first ... at first we would kiss and that was enough. We'd go on these long walks and hold hands and he'd push the hair out of my eyes and he'd kiss me so tenderly. So softly. It was like a fairy tale. Perfect. Everything was perfect.

But then, kissing wasn't enough anymore. For either of us. Things happened really fast then. Every night we'd go further and further until ... well, until I got scared. It was all so strange and exciting and confusing.

I didn't know if I was in love or what. But I was scared. I got scared.

And that's when I told him we needed to slow down.

"Why?"

"To make sure it's real," I said.

"Of course it's real," he said.

He didn't wanna slow down. He didn't wanna stop, and I didn't wanna lose him. So I let him keep going. I mean, when you love someone ... how far should you go in showing 'em you love 'em? How far is too far?

What do you see when you look in the mirror?

What do you see in your eyes and your face?

I see the past like a tower before me.

Oh, who has the keys ... the keys, to this place?

Notes for the Actress

Once again, alter your voice as you remember the song lyrics.

Remember this flashback of the early days of your relationship fondly. Those were good times, before things got out of hand.

You might have been in love — you're not sure — but you became confused and frightened by what was happening.

Basically, this guy raped you. You were scared and alone and he forced himself on you. And now you don't know what to do, because you thought you might have loved him.

After reciting the lyrics, reach out and touch the image of your face in the mirror. Then freeze as the lights fade to black.

Ideas for the Speaker:

(After the lights have faded and BRIDGET has exited, walk On-stage and face the audience. Then, as the lights come back up, say something like ...)

Bridget got caught in a bad place and things went way, way too far. Now her choices and wounds haunt her ... What about you? What do *you* see when you look in the mirror? What haunts you? Have you gone too far? Has someone gone too far with you? Have you stepped over the line? Have you ever wished you could just erase the past? We can't undo what's been done, but we can find forgiveness and love and acceptance in the eyes of God.

Jesus forgives you. Jesus accepts you as is, with all the regrets and baggage and hurts and heartaches. For the wounds you've received and the ones you've caused, Jesus has the keys, the keys to that place.

What do you see when you look in the mirror? When you have faith in Christ, God sees the pure and perfect reflection of his Son.

The good news of Christ is that you can have a second chance. That's what grace is all about. You can receive forgiveness. Yes, you can start again. *(End with prayer.)*

(If the setting is appropriate, you may need to talk about the seriousness of date rape. Direct students to a local Christian counseling service or a hotline that they can call if they need to. Make sure they know what steps to take if someone tries to keep going with them after they've said "No.")

Verses to Check Out:

- "What this means is that those who become Christians become new persons. They are not the same anymore, for the old life is gone. A new life has begun! All this newness of life is from God, who brought us back to himself through what Christ did. And God has given us the task of reconciling people to him" (2 Corinthians 5:17–18).
- "And since we died with Christ, we know we will also share his new life" (Romans 6:8).
- "He heals the brokenhearted, binding up their wounds" (Psalm 147:3).

12. Razor's Edge

Summary:

Ariel has started cutting herself (i.e. "self-inflicting," as those who actually do it refer to it). The pain inside her heart seems so terrible and overwhelming that she has been searching for ways to make it more tangible and manageable.

Purpose:

We all have different ways of trying to cope with our problems, ways of running from difficulties that seem too big and daunting, and ways of trying to fill the holes and emptiness in our lives. By hearing about one girl's specific struggle, you can bridge into a discussion about all the different destructive ways we try to handle our problems rather than bringing our lives to Jesus.

Time:

Five to six minutes

Props/Set:

A scrapbook and scrapbooking supplies, an X-Acto Knife, a chair, and a small table on which to place the supplies

Topics:

Addictions, brokenness, coping, cutting, depression, desperation, emptiness, loneliness, pain, scars, secrets, self-image, self-mutilation, traps

Cast:

You're Ariel, a sixteen-year-old girl who has started self-inflicting (specifically, cutting your left forearm with razor blades). You're lonely, hurting, desperate, and trying to cope, but you just don't know how.

Notes:

Encourage your actress to do some online searches on cutting and self-mutilation to better understand the motives and feelings of those who do self-inflict. Be aware that this drama is pretty intense and graphic and could be quite disturbing to some students. Use discernment about when and where you use it.

ARIEL: Last year I started keeping these scrapbooks. I know it's a lot easier to do it all on the computer, but this seems more ... permanent. All these pictures of my family and friends and stuff ... All these smiling perfect pictures. You can just cut out the parts you don't like. They call it "cropping the photograph."

(Sigh) I liked it better when we lived in Oklahoma, out in the country. Before my dad got this new job. Before we became so ... successful. Before Dad started working so much and Mom got so busy helping out at our church and I got so ... lost in the shuffle.

You'd never guess how I feel, looking at our perfect lawn and perfect house and nice deck and big stupid dog on the porch. You'd never guess it, seeing all that. Picture perfect.

But it's all a shell. Hiding the pain inside.

I guess I first thought about it when I saw this movie about a girl who was into cutting herself. She was making out with her boyfriend when he felt these scars on her arm.

He's like, "What's this? What happened?" And before she could stop him, he pulls up her sleeve. And there, she's got, like, a dozen scars, right? Straight cuts, all in a row. Each one, about two inches long.

She's like, "I cut myself sometimes, all right!" And she pulls down her sleeve.

He's like, "Why?"

And she says something like, "Well, I don't know why, OK? It's just that sometimes it hurts so bad on the inside I need to do something. And I don't know what to do. So ..."

And he says, "So you cut yourself?"

And she's like, "Yeah. It's like crying, or

Notes for the Actress

As the lights come up, you're sitting On-stage. Cut out some of the pictures with the knife. Then begin.

Pause after the opening paragraph.

When you talk about your life being "picture perfect," tilt your scrapbook toward the audience.

As you say "It's all a shell," twirl the knife between your fingers. Pause before transitioning into the story about the movie you rented.

Go back and forth between the two characters, retelling this scene naturally, taking on the voice inflections of the two people.

Notes for the Actress

Be sure you say the line "I know that part … " in Ariel's character, rather than with the inflection and mannerisms of the girl from the movie.

As you quote the girl from the movie, twirl the knife in your fingers again.

Say this comment about the pain getting in softly, more to yourself than to the audience.

This section in which you describe the act of self-inflicting is intense. It should send shivers through the audience.

Use this interlude before describing the cutting as a way of sustaining the suspense.

screaming, but without the tears or without the noise. When you ache this much inside, you gotta find a way to let it out."

I know that part word for word. I kept rewinding it. I memorized it.

Then, after a long pause, he asks, "Does it help?"

And she doesn't answer. She just leans over and pulls him close.

I guess I thought, "Nothing else I've tried has worked. Maybe this will. *"Sometimes it hurts so bad on the inside I need to do something. … When you ache this much you gotta find a way to let it out … "*

If only there was a way to stop it from getting in.

So, I bought some razor blades, I went up to my room, and locked the door — there are some things you only do behind closed doors.

I didn't really know how to do it, so I just sorta set the blade against my left arm. My fingers were shaking. My heart was totally pounding. It all felt scary and exciting and dangerous at the same time. I didn't know if it would help or not. Who knows?

Some people use drugs, right? Some drink. Others use sports or dieting or work or sex or whatever. We all have our ways of trying to cope. Of trying to fill the holes inside.

One of my teachers at school told us about this "fight or flight" thing. I guess when you face dangerous situations, you either stand up and fight, or you try to run away. Some kind of survival instinct or something. I don't know. But I don't think that goes far enough. It's not just dangerous situations you gotta deal with. It's everyday life.

74

And we all have ways of running away from that ...

The blade felt cool and biting. But strangely soothing, too. I watched my skin crease under it. And then ... I pressed down ... and pulled. Blood eased out from around the blade, but I didn't really feel any pain. Not right then. The pain came later.

I set down the razor blade and looked at my arm.

Then, more blood. It was messier than I thought it'd be. I grabbed a T-shirt from my drawer and held it there. The cut was pretty deep. *That'll leave a scar,* I thought. ... And it did.

Once you press down and pull, everything is real. Everything is visible. It all comes to the surface.

Some people call it "self-mutilation." But you're not mutilating yourself. Other people have already done that for you. You're just making the pain a little more visible.

If only there was a way to stop it from getting in. ... *(Optional ending place)*

Anyway, that's what I do to try and escape. To cope, I guess ... I guess you could say it's my drug.

So ... what's yours?

Notes for the Actress

When you retell this episode of cutting yourself, stare into the distance as if you're remembering.

After saying "I thought" and before saying "And it did," feel your forearm where the scar is.

Before closing up, cut a few pictures out before saying, "Anyway, that's what I do ... " Then stare directly at the audience for that last line. Freeze. Fadeout.

75

Ideas for the Speaker:

(As the lights fade and ARIEL exits, walk On-stage and face the audience. Then, as the lights come back up, say something like ...)

We all have our ways, don't we? Our ways of trying to fill the gaps in our hearts and quiet the pain in our souls. Our ways of trying to escape, to cope. But all these ways of running away don't solve anything. They just add more pain. And more scars.

The girl in the monolog asked a good question: What's your drug? What do you do to cope or escape your problems? Drinking? Sex? Porn? Sports? Or do you take your problems to Jesus? He's the one who said, *"Come to me, all of you who are weary and carry heavy burdens, and I will give you rest. Take my yoke upon you. Let me teach you, because I am humble and gentle, and you will find rest for your souls. For my yoke fits perfectly, and the burden I give you is light"* (Matthew 11:28–30).

Let's go to him right now. Let's stop running. Let's stop pretending. Let's stop hiding. And let's let ourselves be found. Bring him whatever you need to bring him. Ask him for help and healing and the courage to stop running. Let his Spirit give your soul the rest and hope it needs. *(End with prayer.)*

Verses to Check Out:

- *"He personally carried away our sins in his own body on the cross so we can be dead to sin and live for what is right. You have been healed by his wounds!"* (1 Peter 2:24).
- *"Don't act thoughtlessly, but try to understand what the Lord wants you to do. Don't be drunk with wine, because that will ruin your life. Instead, let the Holy Spirit fill and control you"* (Ephesians 5:17–18).
- *"The LORD is close to the brokenhearted; he rescues those who are crushed in spirit"* (Psalm 34:18).

13. Fractures

Summary:

Jason broke his arm doing a stupid stunt. Now, as he tells the humorous story of his accident, both he and the audience begin to realize that there are many different kinds of scars.

Purpose:

Use this lighthearted drama to get your audience thinking about the wounds and scars that all of us carry, deep down in our hearts. Use it as an opportunity to discuss inner scars and then explain how to bring them to the Great Physician.

Time:

Four to five minutes

Props/Set:

An x-ray of an arm or shoulder, a sling or a cast for Jason's left arm (you could use crutches and references to a broken leg instead, if you want)

Topics:

Abuse, addictions, appearances, brokenness, hiding, hope, masks, scars, secrets, suffering

Cast:

You're Jason, an eighteen-year-old thrill-seeker who has recently broken his arm. You're not exactly a stand-up comic, but you do tend to see the humorous side of life. When you broke your arm, you did lots of research on fractures.

Notes:

We live in a hurting world. No one leaves it unscarred (not even Jesus did!). This drama will present the idea of inner scars and hidden wounds and then allow you the opportunity to follow up with a discussion on the healing and help that Jesus can bring.

Make sure your actor knows how to pronounce *comminuted* — "COM-in-(oo)t-ed" ("oo" as in *boot*).

Contact a doctor at your church and explain that you're doing a drama in which you need to hold up an x-ray of an arm. See if he or she will let you borrow one. Or, search online for "x-ray pictures" and then print a copy of an x-ray onto glossy photo paper. Here's one website that provides x-rays of arms and shoulders: http://www.orthopedic-doctor.com/patient-education.htm (please note, this is not an endorsement of the content of this site, simply a suggestion for research purposes).

JASON: It was Eric's idea. He'd seen this stunt on some TV show and he was like, "Dude, you can do it, man! I'll drive the car and then when I get close, sprint toward the car, run up the hood, and over the top of the car as I drive under you. It'll be *awesome.*"

And I'm like, "Um, why don't I drive the car while you run toward it *like a complete idiot?!*"

And he's like, "Naw, man. It'll be better this way. I saw the show — I know what to do. Trust me!"

It mighta actually worked if he hadn't accelerated to fifty-five miles an hour ... He was supposed to drive *under* me, not *over* me ...

You couldn't tell it was broken by just looking at it. I mean, yeah, it was swollen a little and kinda discolored and everything, but there were no bones sticking through the skin or anything like that. ... Huh ... that would've been cool. Anyway, you had to look inside to see where the fracture was.

There are, like, sixteen different kinds of fractures. Compression fractures are when the bones get crammed together ... avulsion fractures are when a small piece of bone breaks off from where your ligaments attach to the bones ... open fractures are the kind that poke through the skin. ... I had a comminuted fracture. They "often occur with high impact traumas." Comminute means to pulverize something or turn it to powder ... High impact might be good for aerobics, but it ain't good for fractures, I can tell you that ... Yeah. I know all about fractures ... now.

I could write a book on 'em. Maybe a children's book, or a kid's TV show: *Fun with Fractures.* ... "Today, boys and girls, we're

Notes for the Actor

Walk On-stage with crutches or with your arm in a sling.

Pause after saying "Trust me!" Look at your arm and shake your head.

As you talk about looking at your arm, look at it.

After you talk about the bone poking through, think about it for a few seconds and then mention how cool it would have been.

Pace as you explain these fractures and their graphic descriptions.

Comminuted is pronounced "COM-in-(oo)t-ed" ("oo" as in *boot*).

As you talk about the children's book, imitate Mr. Rogers or another children's entertainer.

Notes for the Actor

When you transition to a new thought, it's a natural place to stand, walk, or move in a new direction.

Point to your arm before saying, "So I figure, why not?"

Imitate your teacher's voice, but don't mock her.

Be respectful to Mrs. Pritchard. You're not talking back to her, just making your case.

Say her line a little more reflectively so the audience can see there's more going on here than meets the eye.

going to talk about bones sticking through your skin! Can you say, 'high impact trauma'? Very good, boys and girls! Let's all practice giving fractures! Here are some baseball bats! Pulverizing is fun!"

So they took this x-ray. I'm laying there and this guy walks up. He's wearing this nuclear bombproof lead apron thing. I'm like, "What's all that for?"

He's like, "Protects me from radiation poisoning."

So I'm like, "OK, where's mine?"

"Oh. We don't give them to the patients."

And I'm thinkin', *No, you wouldn't wanna do that. It might actually* stop *us from growing an extra radiation-induced eyeball under our tongues!*

I guess it keeps 'em in business.

(Sigh) So we got this English assignment, right? We're supposed to write a story about a scar we have. … So I figure, why not?

Afterward, my teacher is like, "You wrote a good essay, but you didn't write about a scar."

And I'm like, "But Mrs. Pritchard, all the damage was on the inside where you can't see it. Not all scars are visible. Trust me, the bone was broken — a comminuted fracture — I can show you the x-ray from Mr. We-Don't-Give-'Em-to-the-Patients."

Then she's all quiet. And she repeats what I said. "Not all scars are visible … "

I wonder what she was thinking.

Anyway, I got an A on the assignment. And the doc says my arm's gonna heal up pretty good. So that's all good. Eric's got another idea. Something about a bungee cord, a skateboard, and a Mack truck. This time, I'm drivin' ...

Broken bones. You can set 'em. You can fix 'em. They heal — eventually. The scars fade. Coupla months, it'll be back to normal. Well ... almost normal. It'll never be quite the same. That's how these things work. That's one of the deals when you get fractured. You're never *quite* the same again ...

Hmm ... "Not all scars are visible."

I wonder what she was thinking ...

Notes for the Actor

After saying "The scars fade," swing your arm around to show it's healing.

Let those last words linger in the air as you exit and the lights fade.

Ideas for the Speaker:

(As JASON exits, walk On-stage and face the audience. Then, as the lights come back up, say something like ...)

We all have scars, don't we? Not only on the outside, but on the inside, too. We tend to look at people's outward appearance. But God looks deep down into your heart and your life, and he sees what's really going on. He sees what your true character is like. There's no playing games with him. No hiding. Or posing. Or pretending. He also knows about all your scars.

God keeps track of all your tears. Did you know that? Psalm 56:8 says, *"You keep track of all my sorrows. You have collected all my tears in your bottle. You have recorded each one in your book."*

God has recorded every scar, every tear, every disappointment in his heart. God cares that much about you. No, we're never quite the same after we've been scarred — even Jesus carried scars on his perfect body — but the pain does fade.

All of us suffer in this hurtful and hurting world. All of us have scars that we carry from thoughtless words that were said ... from cruel deeds that were done ... from unwise choices that we made. God knows about all that. He wants to comfort us and then use us to help comfort others in similar ways. Sometimes God uses the scars in one person's life to help heal similar wounds in another's.

Paul wrote about this in his second letter to the church in Corinth:

"So when we are weighed down with troubles, it is for your benefit and salvation! For when God comforts us, it is so that we, in turn, can be an encouragement to you. Then you can patiently endure the same things we suffer. We are confident that as you share in suffering, you will also share God's comfort" (2 Corinthians 1:6–7).

The God of comfort wants to comfort you right now. He knows your scars. Will you bring them to him and let his Spirit heal your past and touch your life? *(End with prayer.)*

Verses to Check Out:

- *"Cast all your anxiety on him because he cares for you"* (1 Peter 5:7, NIV).
- *"O LORD, do not rebuke me in your anger or discipline me in your rage. Have compassion on me, LORD, for I am weak. Heal me, LORD, for my body is in agony. I am sick at heart. How long, O LORD, until you restore me?"* (Psalm 6:1–3).
- *"Come, let us return to the LORD! He has torn us in pieces; now he will heal us. He has injured us; now he will bandage our wounds"* (Hosea 6:1).

14. We Called Him a Queer

Summary:

Damon remembers picking on a kid who acted differently. Now he regrets the cruel things he said.

Purpose:

Use this drama to initiate discussions on either compassion for others or homosexuality and the issues of acceptance, prejudice, hatred, and tolerance that swirl around it.

Time:

Three to four minutes

Props/Set:

A pile of wooden crosses and sandpaper, or nails and leather cord to make cross necklaces

Topics:

Abuse, belonging, fitting in, friendship, homosexuality, identity, judging others, loneliness, picking on people, prejudice

Cast:

You're Damon, a sixteen-year-old guy who used to call one boy who attended your youth group a "queer." You knew he was lonely and needed a friend, but you were so turned off by his mannerisms that you labeled him "gay" and made fun of him. You're not heartlessly cruel, you just kinda go along with what others are saying or doing. Now you regret treating him as you did.

Notes:

This monolog ends with a bit of a twist as it hints that the boy whom Damon mocked and made fun of was really Jesus in disguise (see Matthew 25:31–46). It's subtle, but it's brought out more clearly in the follow-up discussion.

Throughout this monolog, Damon is either whittling or sanding wooden crosses, or making nail-cross necklaces on leather lanyards. His youth group is going to sell them to make money for a mission trip to Jamaica.

DAMON: Our youth group is selling these things. Doing another fundraiser for a mission trip we're going on. Another mission trip.

To the beach. To Jamaica, mon ...

Another mission trip. ... *(Pause)*

I think his name was Jon. It's hard to remember since he only came to our youth group for the first part of last year.

I knew he wouldn't last. At our church, you have to act a certain way to be cool. To fit in. It's probably that way at a lot of other churches, too.

Anyway, let's call him Jon.

He was easy to make fun of. I mean, the way he stood and the way he moved and that thing he did when he, like, gestured with his hands. It wasn't exactly the way a guy should do it, if you know what I'm talking about. There are different ways to stand and move. And they say two different things about who you are. ...

He told us he was a model for whatever, _____ *(Insert the name of a popular clothing company)*, or something like that, he'd been in two of their magazines. *(Shake your head.)* That only made things worse. We imitated him, the way he spoke and the way he stood and the way he acted. We did it behind his back and we did it so he could see us, too. We *wanted* him to see us.

And we called him names. We called him a lot of names. But mostly, we called him ... well ... I think you can guess. ...

Once Les and I were talking about this girl who was a year older than us and how bad we both wanted to go out with her. She was so hot. And Les was like, "Not you, though, huh, Jonny boy? Right? You'd wanna go out

Notes for the Actor

Hold up an example of the craft project your youth group is selling. When you say "Jamaica, mon" say it in a Jamaican accent.

You want your audience to feel a little uncomfortable when you say this stuff about fitting in.

Imitate these different ways of moving, talking, and standing.

It's OK if you get the audience to laugh here. It'll be uneasy laughter as they realize they really *shouldn't* be laughing.

Talk through this section naturally and easily, taking on the voice and mannerisms of Jon and Les as you tell the story.

85

Notes for the Actor

with another guy, wouldn't you?"

And there was this awkward silence and then Jon looks over at me and then at Les. Maybe to see if I was asking the question, too, or ... maybe to see if I'd do anything to defend him. But I didn't say anything.

"No, I like girls," he said, finally.

"Yeah, right," said Les.

Then Les leans really close to him and says, "You're gay, aren't you, Jonny boy?"

And Jon looked at me and he hesitated. Then he shook his head no.

"Yeah, right," said Les.

After you mention that you didn't really do anything, work on the crosses for a bit before continuing.

And I just stood there and didn't really do anything. ... *(Pause)*

And then one day he was gone. He just didn't come back. Stopped coming to our church altogether.

Nobody said exactly why, but we knew. We'd made him leave. He left because of what we said.

Yup. Another mission trip. We always go somewhere far away for our mission trips. ...

I wonder whatever happened to that kid ... to Jon?

When you say "I know it started with a *J*," look at the cross you're working on.

At least I think his name was Jon. I know it started with a *J*. ...

Huh.

Keep whittling or working on the crosses as the lights fade out.

I wonder what that kid's name really was ...

Ideas for the Speaker:

(After the lights have faded and DAMON has exited, walk On-stage and face the audience. Then, as the lights come back up, say something like …)

And Jesus will say, *"I tell you the truth, whatever you did not do for one of the least of these, you did not do for me"* (Matthew 25:45, NIV). The least of these come in lots of different shapes and sizes. Sometimes they look like the starving kids on those TV ads … sometimes they look like that bum on the street corner … *(Use discernment and tact when listing these categories so that you don't single out a specific student in your group by listing something that he or she would be self-conscious for resembling)* … sometimes they look like the short geeky kid with all the acne … but in each case, in a mysterious way, it's Jesus in disguise.

How have you been treating him?

(Optional section, if you desire to address the issue of homosexuality)

Now, let me mention this. Regardless of the creative interpretations of some people, the Bible clearly calls both homosexual desire and homosexual activity a sin. *(See the verses at the end of this chapter.)* Yet it can be forgiven, overcome, and controlled, just like any other sin.

Those who have a weakness in this area need to be loved and forgiven just as much as those who show prejudice against them. And for all too many of us, that's the bigger issue. That's the one we struggle with. *(End of optional section.)*

Believers are called to love others into the kingdom. That's how we show our love for Jesus. And all too often, there are certain people we'd rather not show love to.

Compassion. It needs to be lived out in the real world in real ways. Because you never know when Jesus himself might just show up in the clothes of the people you like to look down on.

They also will answer, "Lord, when did we see you hungry or thirsty or a stranger or needing clothes or sick or in prison, and did not help you?"

He will reply, "I tell you the truth, whatever you did not do for one of the least of these, you did not do for me."

Then they will go away to eternal punishment, but the righteous to eternal life (Matthew 25:44–46, NIV).

Notes to the Speaker:

Homosexuality certainly is a hot-button issue in churches today. Some churches condone it, others condemn it. In all of the emotion surrounding it, it's important to remember that there's a difference between accepting someone and approving of his or her behavior. We're called to accept people just as God has accepted us: *"So accept each other just as Christ has accepted you; then God will be glorified"* (Romans 15:7). But that doesn't mean we have to approve of how they act all the time.

We can't, in good conscience, approve of sin any more than God can. But even though we all sin, God accepts us, loves us, and welcomes us with open arms. We should do the same with others. The church should be the place where people who struggle with sin — *any sin* — find the most accepting, forgiving, and loving community in all of society. But too often they find the opposite instead. Things will only change when we see people through the eyes of Jesus rather than through the eyes of prejudice, favoritism, or pride.

Verses to Check Out:

- *"My dear brothers and sisters, how can you claim that you have faith in our glorious Lord Jesus Christ if you favor some people more than others?"* (James 2:1).
- *"Do not practice homosexuality; it is a detestable sin"* (Leviticus 18:22).
- *"The penalty for homosexual acts is death to both parties. They have committed a detestable act and are guilty of a capital offense"* (Leviticus 20:13).
- *"Even the women turned against the natural way to have sex and instead indulged in sex with each other. And the men, instead of having normal sexual relationships with women, burned with lust for each other. Men did shameful things with other men and, as a result, suffered within themselves the penalty they so richly deserved"* (Romans 1:26b–27).

15. Why I Flunked Gym Class

Summary:

After Gabrielle's dad saw her report card, she got in trouble. But her dad has no idea what the real problem is.

Purpose:

Use this drama to facilitate a discussion about either drug use or secret sins. Everyone involved with drugs ends up lying, covering his tracks, hiding, and making excuses for his behavior. But it's not just drug users who do that. All of us do the same things when we get entangled in, or addicted to, a sin we don't want anyone else to know about.

Time:

Three to four minutes

Props/Set:

Make sure that Gabrielle is wearing long sleeves or a jacket. She should be dressed like a hard-rocker or goth girl.

Topics:

Addictions, choices, consequences, coping, drugs, emptiness, hiding, masks, secrets

Cast:

You're Gabrielle, a fifteen-year-old goth girl who has been doing drugs for the last few years. You've gotten pretty good at hiding your problem. You're not ready to admit that you need help, nor are you ready to make a change in your life. You're a tough kid. You skip school when you want to, dress like you want to, and listen to hard rock screamer-band music.

Notes:

Gabrielle should dress the part, but don't get so carried away that she becomes comical or a stereotype. She should have a rougher appearance and a harder edge to her. She's tough. She's a survivor.

Even if your audience can't identify with her specific problem (drugs), they'll be able to relate to the more general issue of covering up their sins — whatever those might be.

GABRIELLE: There's lots of kids at school who don't dress like me or listen to the bands I like or anything. They *think* they're s-o-o-o-o-o-o different. They're all so much better than me. But they're not so different. Not really. ...

So I get home from school last month, right? And my dad meets me at the door. He got my report card in the mail — they don't send 'em home with the kids anymore, for obvious reasons — and he's all, like, "What's this about?"

And I'm like, "What's what about?"

And he's like, "How can anyone flunk gym class?"

And I guess it *is* pretty lame, if you think about it. Of all the classes you can flunk and feel good about, gym class is not one of 'em. I mean, physics, sure. Algebra, why not? History, no big deal. But gym class?!

I don't know. I made up some dumb excuse. Like, that I'm not very good at soccer and that we did soccer all semester, or something like that. And my dad bought it. He cussed at me a few times, shook his head, and then just stomped off. *(Pause)*

But the thing is, I just didn't show up. I skipped. ... I've got my reasons.

You see, we got this new phys ed teacher, right? And he's got all these rules. Dress codes and stuff. What you can and can't wear to gym class.

He doesn't let you wear long sleeves.

And I have to wear long sleeves so people don't see ... see my arms, OK?!

I don't know when I started. Maybe eighth grade. Seventh. Who knows? *(Pause)*

Notes for the Actress

You don't like it when people look down on you.

You're annoyed at your dad and he's upset with you — not a good combination for effective communication.

Laugh at yourself a little here. It is pretty sad when you flunk gym class.

You don't have a very supportive family or a very positive home life.

Here you're blaming your physical education teacher for your failure.

You want the audience to wonder why you wear those long sleeves — what it is you might be hiding.

You can see the needle marks when I don't wear long sleeves. My parents don't know. They're pretty much clueless. Mom almost walked in on me once when I was shooting up in my bedroom. But she didn't see. No one sees. No one knows.

Anyway, that's why I flunked gym class.

And that's why my dad yelled at me. And that's how it goes.

I'm getting better at hiding these days. But I still wear long sleeves. You can't be too careful.

I guess we've all got our dirty little secrets, huh? And our own ways of covering 'em up and hiding 'em from the world.

Yup. You and I, we're not so different. The music, maybe. The clothes. The look. But we're not that different, you and I. Not when you really think about it. What do you do when no one's looking? C'mon. We've all got our secrets.

I just wear long sleeves to cover up mine. How far do you go to cover up yours?

Ideas for the Speaker:

(As GABRIELLE exits, walk On-stage and face the audience. Then, as the lights come back up, say something like …)

There's no hiding from God. No secrets with him.

In his letter to the believers in Rome, Paul mentioned that part of the gospel message is Christ's return and the final judgment for sins. All sins. Even secret ones: *"The day will surely come when God, by Jesus Christ, will judge everyone's secret life. This is my message"* (Romans 2:16).

Yeah, God *"knows the secrets of every heart"* (Psalm 44:21). How does that make you feel? Comforted or afraid? The girl in the drama mentioned that we all have our dirty little secrets … was she right? If so, what does that tell you about your need for God's forgiveness? Some people go to great lengths to cover up their sins. How far would you go to see them *forgiven*? Would you go all the way to the cross? Jesus did. For you.

He'll forgive. He'll forget. He'll set you free. Go to him right now. Pull up your sleeve, whatever it is. Stop hiding. Let's pray.

Verses to Check Out:

- *"God will judge us for everything we do, including every secret thing, whether good or bad"* (Ecclesiastes 12:14).
- *"I have never turned away a stranger but have opened my doors to everyone. Have I tried to hide my sins as people normally do, hiding my guilt in a closet?"* (Job 31:32–33).
- *"It is shameful even to talk about the things that ungodly people do in secret"* (Ephesians 5:12).

16. Skin Deep

Summary:

Angie and her friend Jamie grew up together. Now, as their lives are moving in different directions, Angie is reflecting on the things that have changed and the ones that haven't. She's especially concerned about Jamie's destructive obsession with her appearance. But how do we escape the trap of pursuing outward beauty rather than inner integrity?

Purpose:

Use this drama to encourage students to reflect on true beauty and the skewed emphasis that our culture places on outward appearances. Also, this monolog will help teens see that they, too, often fall into the same trap of trying to look good rather than be good.

Time:

Six minutes

Props/Set:

Fashion magazines, a chair, and a small table (optional)

Topics:

Acceptance, appearances, beauty, body image, eating disorders, friendship, growing up, identity, masks, popularity, self-image, traps

Cast:

You're Angie, a seventeen-year-old girl who has seen the destructive forces of an obsession with outward appearance destroy your friend, Jamie, who has an eating disorder. You're still trying to sort out what all this means to you. You wish you could just be real and be accepted for who you are, without having to play all the games of impressing others, being popular, and "making a good impression." You wish that were the case, but you keep playing the games anyway, because you can't seem to break free from the trap of basing your self-image on how you look rather than on who God made you to be.

Notes:

Many complex issues arise in this honest, moving drama — growing up, eating disorders, self-esteem, maturity, friendship, the inevitability of change, life, body image and identity, obsessions, masks, traps, and more. Let the myriad issues add depth to the monolog, but don't feel like you need to discuss or tackle all of them. That would be counterproductive. Instead, simply present the sketch in a genuine way and let the audience apply its truths wherever they're at.

Not all students struggle with eating disorders, but all students are concerned about their appearance. So, by targeting your group discussion on the general issues of body image, beauty, and identity, you can help more students connect with this story and apply it to their lives.

Notes for the Actress

Pick up the fashion magazines, page through them, and then shake your head and begin the drama.

You're really interweaving three stories at once:
1. Jamie's story
2. Your story
3. Emily and Torrie's story.

Keep your gestures, tone, and posture consistent for each story.

As you talk about the fashion magazines, hold up your copies of the magazines. Even though you despise them, you still find yourself paging through them.

Change is inevitable in life, but still you wish you could have remained closer friends.

ANGIE: I work a lot. Baby-sitting, mostly. That, and lifeguarding at the water park in the summers.

So, last night I'm baby-sitting these two girls, right? They're six and four: Emily and Victoria — I call her Torrie. So they wanna play dress-up and they want me to do their hair ... and their nails ... and the four-year-old, Torrie, she's all, "Do my toesies! Do my toesies! I'm a princess!" And she's sticking her feet right in my face.

And it made me think of Jamie.

She's been my friend ever since we were, like, Emily's age. Six or so. When we were kids we played dress-up, too, pretending we were princesses and rock stars and actresses, and then, when we got older, we had all these sleepovers out in this tree house her dad built for her. We'd stay up all night talking about boys, and soccer ... and boys ... and our parents ... and boys ... and school and, well ... boys ... and boys ... and ... boys.

So in junior high *(Or middle school)* she started reading these magazines. You know the ones — with the perfect people. The ones that make you look ugly. And fat. With articles like, "Four Sure-Fire Ways to Tell if Your Boyfriend Is Cheating on You!" or "382 Must-Have Outfits for Fall!" or, like, "Tummy-Trimming Secrets for Summer!" Stuff like that.

When we were kids, Jamie lived down the street, but in the ninth grade, they moved across town and we ended up going to different high schools.

For a while we'd get together on the weekends, you know, but we started making new friends. We had different schedules. Different priorities. Different lives ...

Torrie and Emily are so cute. They always want to be lovely. Pretty. Noticed. Emily's subtle about it. She's all, "How does my hair look?"

And I'm like, "Great."

Torrie, the four-year-old, she's not so subtle. "Look at me!" she says, "I'm pretty!" And she goes running around the house screaming, "I'm pretty! I'm pretty! I'm pretty!"

I wonder when we stop believing that?

So I heard Jamie made the cheerleading team. No surprise there ... *(Pause)* She'd been, like, trying to lose weight forever. Trying to look perfect. She was always gorgeous. But she wanted to be perfect.

Then she collapsed one night at practice. Her mom called to tell us she was in the hospital.

So I went to see her, and she didn't even really look like herself or anything. She'd lost so much weight.

I'm like, "Hi, Jamie."

And she says, "Hi, Angie."

And I just didn't know what to say, so I sat there for a while and then I just held her hand. And she smiled. She even giggled a little. Just like she used to when we were close.

When we were kids.

And there in the hospital, all those sleepovers seemed like they happened a really long time ago. Like they were from another life or something.

Then we talked about the old times back when we were kids and the games we played and the dreams we had about growing up and the boys we used to like ...

Notes for the Actress

As you switch the narrative back to Torrie and Emily, make it a bit more lighthearted once again.

Q: When do we start doubting that God made us each uniquely beautiful?
A: When we start comparing ourselves with other people.

Be more serious now. Jamie's problem is no laughing matter.

These memories are bittersweet. Life moves on, and that's both a good thing and a bad thing — sometimes new problems arise from old, unresolved issues.

Notes for the Actress

You're ashamed to admit it, but you're just like Jamie.

You're trying to make sense of everything, but you're confused.

and how much they'd changed. How much we'd changed. Everything had changed.

We talked until there wasn't anything left to say.

"What happened?" I said, finally.

"I'm too fat," she said.

"You're not too fat," I said. "You're pretty. You've always been so beautiful."

And that's when she started to cry. I sat there with her for a long time.

And when I left, we told each other we'd stay in touch. And we did. For a while. But then we both got busy with our lives. She went away for the summer. To her grandma's place in Colorado, I guess. Her parents thought a summer away would do her good. You know, out in the country, riding horses and stuff. I don't know.

I got a job working at the water park. Lifeguarding. Watching little kids splash around with their moms. ... And yeah, I admit it — watching the guys watch me. ... *(Pause)*

Everyone says character and personality are really what matter most. I say if that's true, then why don't we have personality contests instead of beauty contests? No matter what people say, the reality is that it's all about how you look ... not who you are. *(Pause)*

Jamie was in the hospital again in July. Her grandma didn't really notice anything was wrong, even though Jamie wouldn't wear shorts.

I guess she's gonna be OK. That's what they say. ...

You notice who's in good shape at a water park. You can't help it. I mean, you can see who looks really good in a swimsuit and who doesn't. Everyone notices. You can't help it. ...

I mean, there's nothing wrong with wanting to look good, right? There's nothing wrong with that. Is there?

So all summer I couldn't help thinking about how much better I'd look if I lost a little weight.

I baby-sit again tonight. I guess Emily and Torrie will wanna play dress-up again. I wonder when it'll stop being fun for 'em. When it'll stop being a game. When they'll stop playing dress-up and start living it ... Like Jamie.

And me.

And you.

Notes for the Actress

You struggle with the same things as Jamie. You never really thought about it before, but you do.

Let those last two words hang in the air as you walk Off-stage and the lights fade to black.

Ideas for the Speaker:

(As ANGIE exits, walk On-stage and face the audience. Then, as the lights come back up, say something like ...)

How much makeup would it take for you girls to look the way you want? How much weight would you need to lose? How many new outfits would it take until you're satisfied with how you look? What about you guys — how many hours at the gym is it gonna take before you'll be happy? How many trips to the mirror practicing looking cool before you get it just right?

Whether it's playing the beauty queen or the bodybuilder or the track star or the good student or the goth goddess, it's all dress-up. Illusion. Disguise. And why do we do it? Well, to feel good about ourselves, to be popular, to get people to like us.

Is there anything wrong with that?

Here's what Peter writes about inner versus outer beauty for women: *"Don't be concerned about the outward beauty that depends on fancy hairstyles, expensive jewelry, or beautiful clothes. You should be known for the beauty that comes from within, the unfading beauty of a gentle and quiet spirit, which is so precious to God"* (1 Peter 3:3–4). And hey, the examples might be a little different for guys, but the issues are exactly the same.

I'm glad I don't have to impress Jesus. In fact, I couldn't do it even if I wanted to. It's impossible. You can only be honest with him or dishonest with him. You can't hide from him *or* impress him. Here's the choice — be real or play games.

God knows our most secret doubts and fears, our flaws and warts. You can hide 'em from others, but not from him. Yet he accepts us and loves us completely. He's the one who made you the way you are. And what does he think of you? Well, check out Zephaniah 3:17: *"The LORD your God is with you, he is mighty to save. He will take great delight in you, he will quiet you with his love, he will rejoice over you with singing"* (NIV).

When God looks down at you, he breaks into song. That's what God thinks of his children. As long as you try to find happiness in your image or your reputation or the compliments of other people, you'll be trapped in a losing battle. No matter how lovely or rock-solid you look today, time will not be kind to you forever.

But as long as you seek your identity, your fulfillment, your future in Christ, you'll finally find what you're really looking for. *(End with prayer.)*

Verses to Check Out:

- *"Don't lust for her beauty. Don't let her coyness seduce you"* (Proverbs 6:25).
- *"Charm is deceptive, and beauty does not last; but a woman who fears the LORD will be greatly praised"* (Proverbs 31:30).
- *"I praise you because I am fearfully and wonderfully made"* (Psalm 139:14a, NIV).

17. The Delivery Boy

Summary:

Tony fell in love with Raphael's pizza the moment he tasted it. Soon he was telling others about it, delivering pizzas for Raphael door-to-door, and even handing out free samples at a local grocery store. But eventually he became discouraged when people refused to try it for themselves. That's when he went back to his old burger habits. ... Now he's wondering if he made the right choice.

Purpose:

Use this drama get your students thinking about the health (and intimacy) of their relationship with God.

Time:

Seven minutes

Props/Set:

A baseball cap from a pizza restaurant that delivers, a musician's stool

Themes:

Authenticity, belonging, compromise, fitting in, hypocrisy, Jesus, masks, traps, warnings, witnessing

Cast:

You're Tony, a seventeen-year-old guy who was an enthusiastic patron of Raphael's Pizzeria. Eating his pizza completely changed your life! But then, when you started to face tough times and persecution, you gave up on Raphael and his pizzeria and you went back to your old friends and your old, bland fast food. You're dissatisfied and wonder if maybe you should have stuck with Raphael after all ...

During the monolog, the pizza delivery baseball cap represents Raphael and his pizzeria. Your relationship with the hat throughout the drama mirrors your relationship with Raphael — at first you discover it, eventually you put it on, but then you take it off, take one final look at it, and then leave it behind. You're like the seed that fell on the rocky places in Jesus' parable of "The Sower and the Soils." (See Matthew 13:1–9 for Jesus' story and Matthew 13:18–23 for his explanation of it.)

Notes:

This drama is one of the longest ones in the book. It needs to be a little more fleshed out because it tells the complete story of Tony's relationship with Raphael and his pizzeria. Most of the other monologs only tell a portion of, or give a brief summary of, someone's story. As a result, this script will take more time to learn and rehearse.

Whenever Tony talks in the voice of Raphael, he does it with an Italian accent.

To introduce this story, consider having another actor or student from your group read the parable of "The Sower and the Soils" (found in Matthew 13:1–9) aloud to the audience.

As Tony tells this story, he should change his mood to reflect the feelings he had at each specific section of the story.

TONY: I still remember the first time I visited Raphael's Pizzeria.

The moment I bit into that tender crust and took my first bite of his famous Sicilian pizza, I knew my life would never be the same again. The sauce! The cheese! The spicy Italian sausage! Oh! "Mama Mia! That's-a what I call-a pizza!"

I started telling everyone about Raphael's Pizzeria. No matter how much time I spent there, I just couldn't get enough of his pizza! No more soggy fast food or frozen pizzas for me! Now I had the real thing!

Some of my friends asked me, "Who do you think Raphael is, anyway? The greatest chef in the world?"

"Whether he's the greatest chef in the world, I don't know," I said. "But this much I do know: I was hungry and now I'm satisfied. I was starving and now I'm full!"

Anyway, most of the time I'd just invite people to come with me and we'd eat together for an hour or two every Sunday.

"Taste and see that the pizza is good!" I'd tell them.

And they did.

Well, some of them did. Some just shook their heads and called me a pizza fanatic.

But I didn't care because every time I visited Raphael's Pizzeria, I'd taste something new and exciting. And I'd get better acquainted with Raphael, the Master Chef.

Then one day Raphael called me over. "Raphael has a special-a job-a for you," he says. "Raphael needs-a someone to deliver his-a pizza. Yes?!"

I have to admit I was pretty surprised he

Notes for the Actor

Your pizza delivery hat is on a stool at Center Stage as the lights come up. Walk On-stage, look at the hat, pick it up, and begin the monolog.

Don't let this section become too preachy or heavy-handed. You're simply setting the expectation with the audience that this monolog is going to be a parable or an allegory, rather than a "true" story.

Smile as you talk about how exciting it was to hang out with Raphael. Those were good memories.

Whenever you speak for Raphael, do so with an Italian accent.

Notes for the Actor

When you finally agree to deliver pizzas for Raphael, put on the hat and show us that you're excited! It's an honor to work for the Master Chef!

Show by the way that you talk and by your posture that things aren't so rosy anymore.

In this section, imitate the voice and emotion of these three people.

asked me. I mean, I'd only been eating there for a couple months. Who was I to deliver pizzas? I hadn't memorized the menu! I didn't know all there was to know about the restaurant!

"But what if someone asks me a question that I don't know the answer to?" I said. "Like what ingredients you use in the crust, or the secret behind your world-famous, super-spicy sauce?"

"Just-a tell them a-what you know!"

"But what if I deliver a pizza to someone and they don't like it?" I asked.

"No! No! No! You don't a-worry about-a that-a!" Raphael said, pointing to his chest. "You-a leave-a that-a up to me-a! All Raphael wants-a you to do-a is deliver the goods!"

So finally, I agreed. And that afternoon, I was knocking on my first door, delivering pizzas for Raphael.

For a while everything went great as I traveled door to door for Raphael, delivering pizzas. Then, as Raphael's business grew, he asked me to hand out free samples of his pizza at a local grocery store.

So I did … But that's when the trouble started. You see, even though most people were pretty nice when I offered them a free piece of pizza, some of 'em were downright rude.

(Angrily) "I ate pizza when I was a kid," one guy said. "I've had enough to last a lifetime!"

(Like a snob) "My parents used to take me to Raphael's," this one girl told me. "But I didn't like the music, so I stopped going."

(Like a know-it-all) "All pizzas are the same," some people said. "It doesn't matter what brand you eat, as long as you eat something."

"No, Raphael's is different," I explained. "Here, try some!"

But they just refused. And I took it personally.

I talked to Raphael about it. "It's-a not up to you-a to get them to-a like-a me," he said. "Just-a offer them-a free-a samples. That's-a your job!"

I got frustrated because so many people refused the pizza. And some of my friends started ignoring me.

"Ever since you started working for Raphael, you're different," they'd tell me. "It's like the food we eat isn't good enough for you any more. It's like you think you're better than us just because you're hanging out with Raphael these days."

I told them they had it all wrong, but they wouldn't listen. They just made fun of me for standing there handing out those free samples.

And it hurt.

So then I figured maybe I'd just give away *part* of the pizza — you know, like the sausage or cheese — the parts people really like. I started picking off the toppings and handing 'em out one by one.

"Anyone want some pepperoni? I've got a nice handful of it right here! How about some diced onions! They're really quite tasty!"

One day Raphael walked in on me as I was removing all the anchovies with tweezers. "What are you-a doing?!"

"Oh, hey, Raphael. I thought people might be offended by the rest of the pizza, so I'm only giving 'em the parts they like!"

And he's like, "But how will they-a know-a what Raphael's pizza really tastes-a like if you don't-a give them the whole-a piece-a?"

105

Notes for the Actor

Once I got so frustrated with this little kid who refused to try some that I grabbed him by the throat and jammed a piece of pepperoni pizza into his mouth. "Eat this, kid! It's good for you!" I yelled.

I nearly got arrested for that.

"You can't-a force-a someone to-a like-a my pizza," explained Raphael. "They have to be a-hungry before they'll take a bite. If you try a-shoving my-a pizza down-a their throats-a, they'll spit it back-a out-a in your face-a!"

But still, I felt like a failure every time someone turned me down. ...

Well, things are a lot different these days. I gave up working for Raphael a few months ago. And I stopped eating at his pizzeria except for on special occasions like Christmas or Easter.

I'm a lot more popular with my old friends now. Sometimes, from our new hangout at one of the local burger joints, we watch Raphael's delivery boys going door to door.

"Pizza freaks," we say. And take another big bite of our soggy burgers.

(Looks longingly at the hat.) But sometimes, when I'm really hungry and nothing else seems to satisfy me, I think back to what it was like working for Raphael. ... After all, it's been a long time since we've talked, and even longer since I've had any of his pizza. Come to think or it, I can hardly remember what that pizza of his even tastes like.

Huh ... it couldn't have been all *that* good.

Could it?

Ideas for the Speaker:

(The spiritual parallels in this story are pretty evident and will probably be more effective with your audience if you don't spend a lot of time explaining them. Often, the more you explain a story, the less impact it has. Instead, help your teens see themselves in the story and write a better ending with their own lives.

After the lights have faded and the actor exits, walk On-stage and face the audience. Then, as the lights come back up, read the story of "The Sower and the Soils" [found in Matthew 13:1–9]. If you've already read the story to introduce the monolog, you can walk up On-stage and say something like ...)

Jesus said, *"The rocky soil represents those who hear the message and receive it with joy. But like young plants in such soil, their roots don't go very deep. At first they get along fine, but they wilt as soon as they have problems or are persecuted because they believe the word"* (Matthew 13:20–21). There were three other kinds of soil, too. One that never understood the word; one that got distracted by the pursuit of wealth and worldly things; and one that received it, believed, and persevered.

Which soil are you? Where do you show up in this story?

What are you going to do about it today?

Verses to Check Out:

- *"You adulterers! Don't you realize that friendship with this world makes you an enemy of God? I say it again, that if your aim is to enjoy this world, you can't be a friend of God"* (James 4:4).
- *"If you want to be my follower you must love me more than your own father and mother, wife and children, brothers and sisters — yes, more than your own life. Otherwise, you cannot be my disciple"* (Luke 14:26).
- *"Another [potential convert] said, 'Yes, Lord, I will follow you, but first let me say good-bye to my family.' But Jesus told him, 'Anyone who puts a hand to the plow and then looks back is not fit for the Kingdom of God' "* (Luke 9:61–62).

Topical Index

Verse Index

Cast Index

About the Author

Steven James is an award-winning author, popular conference speaker, and creative solo performer. He appears weekly at conferences, churches, schools, and special events around the country sharing his unique blend of drama, comedy, and inspirational speaking. Steven is the author of fifteen books and has spoken more than 1000 times all across North America in the past five years.

When Steven completed his master's degree in storytelling in 1997, there were fewer than 100 people in the world with the same degree. Since then, he has been in demand throughout the country as a conference presenter, family entertainer, youth speaker, and performance storyteller.

Drawing from a diverse background in the performing arts and education, Steven James weaves together programs that touch both the mind and the heart. Through his writing and speaking, he has creatively communicated a message of hope and humor to more than 500,000 people over the last decade.

Steven lives with his wife and three daughters in eastern Tennessee.